Kilfenora, Killinaboy & Scattery Island

A guide for pilgrims in County Clare

Rosemary Power

Keeper

Published 2015 by KEEPER BOOKS
via FeedAread.com – with funding from
the English Arts Council

Copyright © 2015: Rosemary Power

First Edition

A CIP catalogue record for this title is available from the
British Library

Paperbacks and eBooks are available from –

    FeedAread.com
    Amazon.co.uk
    Amazon.com

Booksellers can order from –

    Ingrams; Barnes & Noble; Easons;
    Gardners; Nielsen; Bertrams, Argosy

Cover design & layout: © 2015: David Rice,
Keeper Books / Killaloe Communications
    www.killaloe.ie/kcs
    www.LookAndGrowMindful.com
    www.killaloe.ie/khs

Contents

Foreword 7

Section 1: Kilfenora 13

Section 2: Killinaboy
& south to the estuary   55

Section 3: Scattery Island 93

Conclusions 125

Bibliography 129

Acknowledgements

THANKS are due to many people, who have walked all or part of the route outlined here, or have joined with walks around the sites mentioned. Olive Carey, Kay Muhr and Cathy Swift gave invaluable practical, historical and archaeological advice. Cathy Swift also provided insights into the poetry, and Kay Muhr advised on place-names. Peter Harbison, Michael MacMahon, Risteard Ua Croinín and John Keane read and commented on some sections in draft, and Kevin Griffin and Don MacGahbann allowed me access to their unpublished doctoral theses. Mike O'Neill allowed use of his unpublished summary of Kilfenora and his photographs. The support of Des Bain, Michael Killeen and Frances Connole is gratefully acknowledged. Methodist Home Mission allowed me the time to complete the text. Many people provided insight into Scattery Island and modern perspectives. David Bunney undertook proof-reading. The research was assisted by a small grant from the Centre for Antique, Medieval and Pre-Modern Studies, National University of Ireland, Galway. The errors of fact and interpretation are my own. My chief thanks is to my publisher David Rice of Keeper Books for his immense commitment and effort in bringing this forward to publishing, through his layout, design, comments and suggestions. This book is dedicated to the memory of Chris Power.

Permissions appear on page 139.

Foreword

THIS is intended as a practical guidebook with historical content, for people visiting three major early Christian sites in Ireland, and smaller sites associated with them. One is Kilfenora on the Burren, the starting-point for this guide. The route described here to the south may have formed part of a medieval pilgrim route, but has been adapted for walking today. The route then suggested is for those who wish to continue it south-west to another great early Christian site and place of pilgrimage, Scattery Island.

The first part of the book is mainly a guide round a medieval church and its environs. The second part concerns the stopping places on a route south, ancient sites with the remains of early churches and other evidence of their continual spiritual significance locally. The third is a walk around the ruins on Scattery Island and the written sources associated with its founder saint.

The only, tenuous, link is the founder saint of Killinaboy, which lies on the route suggested, and whose patron has a link with both Kilfenora and Saint Senan of Scattery. Many early Christian saints were linked together in the poetry, Saints' Lives and other works written many centuries after they had died, and in the case of Inghean

Bhaoith, Daughter of Baoith, Innewee, of Killinaboy, the jurisdiction of her church appears in later times to have bordered on that of Kilfenora, which was in the Middle Ages the mother-church of the bishopric. She was also said to be associated through close kinship with Senan of Scattery Island. There are no *Lives* of Fachtnan and Inghean Bhaoith, so they appear shadowy figures from the early Christian period; but there are a number of written accounts from later centuries about Senan.

A much less tenuous link between the saints and their sites is the modern desire to walk in spiritual search or at least for leisure and refreshment, between different sites. This book is intended to be of use to those who do this, and while it remains on-road, it seeks to avoid the busier routes.

People walk between historical sites for many reasons, including exercise, a love of heritage, and the spiritual quest which makes the journey as significant as the arrival. This book cannot hope to serve all these attractions but seeks to provide some practical as well as other less tangible guides for those who wish to explore Ireland, and their own lives, in this manner.

The practical is intended as a bare outline, not a gazetteer of information, for much of this can best be found on the internet, and information will change from season to season. The routes and the main settlements are marked out, and the walker is invited to linger, and to be open to seeming distractions.

A pilgrim walk is about the journey as much as the arrival; and it may be worth spending time in a specific place and seeing what it can offer, in terms of local sites and in terms of specific events. The walk may be undertaken over several seasons, if time is limited. The sense of self, and the companionship gained on the journey may be as important as the arrival.

Where possible, planned walkers' routes such as the Burren and Mid Clare ways have been indicated.

Small pieces of information have been included in boxes, for the walker to use or not. A bibliography is given, of works used, but it is by no means exhaustive and there are many modern local guides that will be of use to understand the history, the plant and animal life, the folklore, and what an area means to some of the people who live in it today.

County Clare has been particularly well served by scholars and antiquarians, in particular John O'Donovan and Eugene O'Curry, who with others worked on the *Ordnance Survey of Ireland*, and had their Letters published in 1839; and the antiquarian James Westropp, who published in the late nineteenth and early twentieth centuries. Much of their work is now available online.

This guide is therefore intended to give some understanding of the historical sites of Kilfenora and Scattery Island, and some of the places between them, in a context that seeks to reflect that these have been places of reverence to people for many generations. These are places where people have stayed, worked and prayed over centuries. There are also many ancient remains in the area that demonstrate the long history of farming the limestone lands of North Clare and the coastal lands to the west and south. In walking it we may find a deepening of our own journey through it, and through life, leaving it pristine but honoured, for the benefit of those who succeed us.

Some of the boxes contain translations of prayers, anecdotes and poems from earlier times. Biblical Psalms are given in the Grail translation, which is intended for communal recitation and singing.

They are offered in this tone, in the hope that, whatever the reason for the walker's journey, it may be enriched and that some of the delight these poems and stories contain may blend with the experience of walking this ancient landscape.

Given as they are in translations into modern English, from older forms of Irish, or from Latin, they are intended

> It is folly for anyone in the world to cease from praising God, when the bird does not cease and it without a soul but wind.
>
> **Irish, eleventh century, trans Jackson, 136, adapted.**

> Learned in music sings the lark,
> I leave my cell to listen;
> His open beak spills music, hark!
> Where heaven's bright cloudlets glisten.
>
> And so I'll sing my morning psalm
> That God bright heaven may give me
> And keep me in eternal calm
> And from all sin relieve me.
>
> **Eighth - tenth century, trans. Flower**

to show something of the content of prayers known to the earlier Christians of Ireland. In particular, they concern those who lived before or during the twelfth century, before most of the stone church buildings were erected. These compositions supplemented the scriptures and other religious works, and have the additional delight of being native works, the product of people's spirituality and artistic ability in this particular land and time. In many cases they have survived because they were copied out later by others who valued them.

The English translations in turn have gone through different stages. Some have the romantic tinge of the Celtic Twilight, and sometimes meanings were only guessed at by the translators of the time. Poems and prayers of this period were also presented in poetic form in English, a habit that has largely died out among modern scholars, but which makes many of the translations poems in their own right. Interspersed are some modern translations, which benefit from the scholarship of the last century which has managed to provide more precise understandings of words and images.

The names of the saints mentioned in the text are given in the Classical Irish forms, as adopted by Pádraig Ó Riain

11

in his recent *Dictionary of Irish Saints*. The local anglicised version is sometimes given as well, especially if it is relevant to a local place-name. The exception is the name Senan, where the modern spelling is used throughout for this well-known Clare saint.

Kilfenora east window – Photo: R. Power

Section One

KILFENORA

AT the heart of the small town of Kilfenora, on the edge of the Burren, is the medieval cathedral church with its associated high crosses. While we have no written accounts of the founder or the early church here, there are physical remains from the middle ages which show us how significant the place was in earlier times.

Kilfenora – the name

The Irish name, Cill Fhionnúrach, 'Church of Fionnúir' comes from the earlier form Cill Fhindabrach. This may

13

mean either the 'church of the white water', or the 'church of the white height'. Similar place-names are found elsewhere in Ireland, usually where there is a hill and often close to water. These places seem to have had a religious significance before the coming of Christianity, and the word finn, 'white', also carries the sense of 'blessed'.

A name containing the word 'white' is very suitable for this site. Kilfenora is situated at the foot of the high Burren (An Boirne, the great rock), the limestone region of North Clare which has a unique plant life and history. The name may refer more specifically to the limestone ridge between the church centre and the great fort at Ballykinvarga about two kilometres away.

The underlying rock of the town itself is a sheet of limestone, which can be seen in some places under the topsoil. It is a patch of fertile land surrounded by poorer quality land, which may have much to do with its importance in ancient times and until relatively recently.

With regard to the name, the 'f' sound disappears in Irish after a feminine word such as cill, church, but it is often restored in modern forms, and it appears too when records were written by those who knew Latin. The nineteenth-century antiquarian Thomas Westropp noted how the name appears in the *Book of Rights*, which deals with the period AD 450-902, as Cathair Fhionnabhrach, while it is Fenabor in 1189, in the genitive as Funbranensis in a Latin text of 1273, and Fenaborens in 1302. The form Cellumabrach, which contains the word 'cill', is also found.

Fionnúir is not a personal name and the saint associated with the site is Fachtna or Fachtnán, often spelt Fachnan in English. He was thought to be an early Christian saint who died in about AD 590. He does not seem to be the same saint as his near-contemporary Fachtna of Cork, a foster-son of Saint Ita of Killeady, also trained by Saint Finbar, and associated with Ross Carbery.(*) There is, however, a story that this Saint Fachtna went blind, and was healed and founded the church at Kilfenora in thanksgiving. This might have been a later attempt to link the better-known saint from the south-west with this Burren foundation, but it fits with the Irish Martyrologies (saints' lists) that name Fachtna as bishop of Ross and Kilfenora. If so, he has travelled far from his place of origin, and it may be that there were two early saints with the same name.

There was was a large monastery at Kilfenora by the end of the early Christian period (c.600 – c.1200). This can be seen from the amount of land enclosed within the remains of the surrounding ramparts, the monastic 'vallum', or 'termon', which marked the boundaries of the sacred space under the protection of the saints and owned by the monastic community.

Whether it came first or whether it was built here because there was a great secular centre of power, at Ballykinvarga nearby, is not known.

The background

The medieval site was, like the early Christian site, dedicated to the saint, Fachnan. By understanding it more, we may be able to journey imaginatively in time to what went before, and to understand more how it changed in later centuries.

This site has been a place of worship for many centuries, and this church has been here for some nine hundred years. There may have been a church here from the sixth

---

* Ó Riain takes them as the same saint. *Dictionary*, 300. Also Westropp, "Lisdoonvarna, Kilfenora and Lehinch", 14.

century, though in the Early Christian period churches were usually small wooden buildings and there were often more than one within a monastic site. There was by the eleventh century a stone church on this site or nearby, because we are told in the *Annals of Inisfallen*, that among many similar acts of warfare, in 1055: 'The stone church of Cell Fhinnabrach was completely burned'. Another fire is thought to have occurred in 1100.

The current roofed building, together with the narrower and now ruined chancel, dates from about the beginning of the thirteenth century. Parts of the nave may be the earliest section of the church to survive: there are some huge stones under the plaster of the west and north walls, a type of 'cyclopean masonry' which is associated with early churches in Ireland.

The Synod of Kells in 1152 established Kilfenora, called Fenabore, as a bishopric of the archdiocese of Cashel, under the new order. Perhaps a stone church had been already begun in anticipation, to prove the significance of the site and that it was capable of sustaining a bishopric. The area was naturally good in agricultural terms, especially cattle-rearing, and there was reason for local people to wish to have, or retain, an older bishopric. This was the principal church site of the Corca Modrúad, the tribe from which we get the English name Corcomroe as in the Cistercian abbey of Corcomroe to the north. The people later paid tribute to their powerful Ua Briain neighbours, whose heartlands were to the south of Clare.

Whether the stone church we see today was started before or after the Synod of Kells, work seems to have progressed quite rapidly. This may have been initiated by a certain F. of Kilfenora, who attended a church council in Limerick in 1205. (*) Another patron and founder may

---

* McCaffrey, *Black Book of Limerick*.

16

The Twelfth-century Irish Church Reform

Ireland received Christianity in the fifth century, best known through the work of the missionary Saint Patrick. It spread during the sixth century, when it also reached the islands and northern mainland of Scotland. (Southwest Scotland and western England had received Christianity in previous centuries.) As a result of cultural differences and isolation, Ireland retained certain practices longer than the continental church, and these sometimes caused friction. Further, although there had been early attempts to organise the Church in Ireland as on continental lines, with bishops based in cities and having authority in the local area, Ireland was a rural society without large settlements. Consequently a monastic-focussed church had developed. While the situation changed over the centuries, the larger monasteries usually had strong links with the local kingdom, and the leader, the abbot or head of the monastery, was often from the ruling kin-group. A bishop who performed sacramental functions resided within many such monastic communities. This led to there being many bishops; and together with certain other practices, like those surrounding marriage, the church in Ireland was looked on with concern by the increasingly centralised universal western church and the papacy. Synods to progress change were held in 1101 and 1111, called by the powerful king Muirchertach Ua Briain (1086-1119), the great -grandson of Brian borúma who died at the Battle of Clontarf in 1014. A further Synod was held in 1152. A more standard European form of church organisation, with fewer bishops and larger territories developed. The continental monastic orders, in particular the Cistercians, were introduced, and the traditional form of monasticism also underwent reform. A large number of stone parish churches were built. Additional changes came after the Anglo-Norman invasion of Ireland in 1170, an event which ultimately led to English rule.

have been the king Donat Ua Bríain, one of the Dál Cais family of Munster monarchs. He built Killaloe Cathedral on the river Shannon in east Clare in the early thirteenth century.(*)

---

[*] Kalkreuter, *Boyle Abbey*, 68.

The outer walls of the current church are rendered, as they would have been in medieval times. They would have been plastered on the inside, using a lime wash, which were then probably covered with long-vanished wall-paintings.

The reasons for building this large church may relate to the twelfth-century restructuring of the Irish church, to conform to continental practice and the dominance of Rome. What we see now is the restructured church, fitted with oak furnishings from the 1840s.

This remains a consecrated church, in the Church of Ireland (Anglican, Episcopalian) tradition, and has been used recently for ecumenical services and community events. For many people it remains a place of great peace. The surrounding churchyard is visited by people with family graves here.

The entrance

Like most medieval churches, Saint Fachnan's is laid out west to east, with the high altar under the east window, pointing to the rising sun and in theory to Jerusalem, the place of Christ's resurrection. It is a reminder, that according to Christian belief, all people will also rise in the body, on the last day. The churchyard is laid out with the headstones facing the east.

The door is the entry into the House of God, the local mother-church; and is representative of the Old Testament pilgrimages which led to the Temple in Jerusalem. This was the Temple for the people of the area.

The door is on the south side of the church. Originally Irish stone churches had west-end doors, as on the Continent. They usually narrowed slightly from the base upwards and were topped by a flat lintel, forming a trabeate doorway. In the twelfth century, the door was often moved to the south-side, perhaps to avoid letting in the rain. Carved arches in the Continental fashion appeared, as it does here.

Over the door, on the outside, is a medieval head, wearing a mitre. This is the first of many fine carvings at the site.

Heads like this would have reinforced the understanding that the cathedral was the seat of a bishop, who ruled with the authority of the church; and stressed continuity between the contemporary church and the original saints who founded the sites for Christian worship.

The role of church and bishop was to continue in a new and authoritative way what was received from the past. The church was the bishop's cathedral, the place of his cathedra, the chair from which he taught.

The head is medieval and could be no earlier than the mid-twelfth century, because it wears a medieval mitre. This head-covering, used on liturgical occasions by bishops and abbots, took the form of points back and front at about this period. Before that a large cap had been worn which tended to develop into points at both sides of the head. They may have looked too much like horns for comfort, so this style was adopted instead.

The porch was formed during a re-structuring of the 1840s. Originally, the door opened straight into the body of the church. In this porch are preserved three grave-stones, which would originally have been laid flat over the body of the deceased. Two of these stood until recently below the east windows in the ruined choir.

The stone figures are of clerics and have been moved inside to preserve them. One appears to date from the thirteenth century and apparently depicts a cleric, with an elaborate close-cropped hairstyle or a small cap with a decorative edge. He has a long, slender neck and something like a collar round it. He is wearing a tunic with a pleated skirt to mid-calf, and close-fitting shoes; and he is holding a book, indicative of learning. The other recumbent figure is a bishop in full liturgical dress, fully robed. He wears a mitre and has his right hand raised in blessing. The upright slab has the incised figure of another bishop, again in full regalia, with an elaborate mitre and vestments, the lower edges of which show a broad band of diamond patterning. One hand is raised in blessing and the other holds an Irish-style crozier. His feet are represented sideways, as if he is walking, which is perhaps intended to show that he was active in the service of God, or even a pilgrim himself.

The quality of these finely-carved images suggests that there was a centre, perhaps a school, for carving in this western cathedral.

On entering, the wall to the left, the west wall, gives some indication of the earlier building. A window can be seen about three metres above the floor, and within the wall there is a small space. This is reached by medieval stairs cut in the thickness of the wall (which are not currently accessible). There are twelve steps up to an open platform, then a further eighteen cut in a spiral. They lead to the small bell-tower visible from the outside, at the top of the strange, stepped, west gable of the church.

While stairs cut in the thickness of medieval walls are not unusual, the opening and platform seem to have had some specific purpose. Further, if Kilfenora followed the Sarum Rite, a medieval liturgy that takes its name from Salisbury cathedral in southern England, it might explain this opening at the west window. A similar arrangement is found in several secular cathedrals, and is associated

20

with a Palm Sunday rite where choirboys sang out through the west gable. (*) This may be a simplified version of the west fronts of St Patrick's Cathedral, Dublin; St. Canice's Cathedral, Kilkenny; or the south transept gable of St Patrick's Cathedral, Cashel. Kilfenora was a suffragan diocese of the archbishopric of Cashel.

Another possibility is that the larger inner window was used to display saints' relics at particular festivals. It would also have served to let natural light in, especially for evening services as the sun was setting. It is also possible that a statue stood there.

From the porch we can see that the cathedral had a high-pitched roof. The current church, which consists of most of the original nave, has excellent sound for the human voice and for instruments.

The door opposite the entrance leads to a small vestry for clergy to robe in, formed from the body of the church during the nineteenth-century restructuring. It occupies one of the original north bays of the church and has its own hearth.

The nave

This part of the church takes its name from the Latin word navis, ship. The medieval nave included the porch area, and the wall and door to the current church. Both date from the restructuring in the nineteenth-century. Originally there was a single structure which included the ruined chancel, the eastern part of the building. The proportions have to be understood from the outside.

---

* Fletcher, 'Liturgy and music in the medieval cathedral', 140-143.; 'The architectural history of the medieval cathedral', 96-119.

21

To imagine the original scale, we need to add the bay that is now the porch and vestry, and also take away the current wall with the Communion area and window, and to look through the slightly narrower chancel to the original east window. The arch holding this wall and window probably contained a roodscreen in the Middle Ages, but the eye is drawn towards the ruined east window, under which would have stood the high altar. There may also have been side-chapels in the bays on the north side of the nave, used for the saying of Masses. However, these bays may have once been arches leading to a side-aisle which has vanished.

There are many layers of change in this building. The nave was the gathering-place in a medieval church for laypeople who attended the services. The walls would have been painted, with scenes from the Bible and other religious stories. There would have been statues, probably wooden ones.

Originally, people stood for services, however lengthy, or brought their own stools, so the cathedral would have had room when needed for several hundred people. There would have been daily services as well as larger Sunday and special liturgical events. The nave was retained as a Church of Ireland parish church, but kept the status of cathedral, even though there was no longer a resident bishop. The 1837 plans of the architect James Pain have survived and are kept by the Church of Ireland's Representative Church Body Library in Dublin.

Kilfenora is a rare example of a medieval cathedral church re-furnished at this time and little changed since. It was slightly restored in the early years of the this century, when new under-floor heating was added.

In the northern wall there are two hearths. The one near the west end is still in use. Nearer the east end on the north wall the minister had a second one.

Neither was part of the medieval building, but they were added in later centuries. A hearth is not required in a church: however it serves to

Kilfenora font – Photo: R. Power

provide warmth and is a focus for informal modern prayer, modelling the way in which the hearth was the centre of the traditional Irish home, where people gathered, the visitor was welcomed, news and stories were told and meals eaten.

Close to the door there is a large medieval baptismal font, carved in limestone, decorated with fluted scallop ornament. It is now on four pillars but there was perhaps once a central one as well, through which the water used in baptism would drain away. The form is typical of the thirteenth century and the style of carving has been compared to that on one of the capitals of the east window, and on the pinnacles of the tower. It may be part of the original furnishings of the church. A late-twelfth-century decree required that parish churches in Ireland have a stone or wooden font, but this is one of relatively few that survive.

The font is traditionally placed near the door of a church. The Sacrament of Baptism is the entry to the Christian life, so the life of faith starts here and progresses to the Communion table, which faces Jerusalem. Possibly the font was once painted. Other services were also held at the entrance to a church, such as the ceremony of churching women after childbirth. This started with the new mother holding a lighted taper at the door of the church and progressing inward.

The floor consists of slabs of Liscannor stone, a local shale from the area close to the Cliffs of Moher. It contains fossils of creatures that swam the seas millions of years ago.

On the north wall is a substantial monument from the late seventeenth century, showing that the arches, if they had ever opened to an aisle, had by then been blocked. This monument was erected in 1685 for members of the MacDonagh family, local Irish landowners. The Latin text below has been translated as:

Remember death. Beauty, popularity, youth and wealth have passed from thee. Learn what is man, after man he becomes a worm, after a worm he becomes stench and horror. So every man changes into what is not man. So passes the glory of the world. Whoever thou shall be who passes by, stand ready and weep. I am what thou shalt be, I have been what thou art, I pray thee pray for me. (*)

Underneath, hidden from sight by the pews, is a further inscription which identifies it also as the tomb of another family member, whose name is given as Dr Patrick MacDonagh. He was a Catholic bishop who died in 1752. Local story has it that all attempts to move the bishop's remains, or others of the family, were strongly resisted, and this situation was finally accepted by the cathedral authorities.

Sometimes funeral monuments like this were used in the Easter Sunday services. Other burials took place over the centuries under the floor.

On the plans of 1837, the pews were intended to stretch to the back on the south side and leave a space on the north side by the hearth, where the font would be placed. This did not happen when the work was done in the 1840s. The back of the church is open space, while the body contains straight-backed fixed oak pews, which congregation members would have rented as part of their commitment to the upkeep of the church, and to present and preserve their local status. As a Protestant church in a largely Catholic country, the numbers attending would probably always have been fairly small.
Near the front are two box-pews – pews with their own doors and with seats all round inside. The likely occupants were the local landowners on one side and on

---

* Quoted Flanagan, *Kilfenora*, 61-2, from a Fr Harrify.

the other the dean and his family. Servants would have been among those who stayed at the back, perhaps bringing their own seating.

The altar area is quite small, but has massive wooden Communion rails, which indicate the significance attached to taking the Sacrament on the relatively rare occasions when this occurred. Inside is a modern Communion table and cross. Although dominated by the huge structures on each side, this is the focus of the church, the place where the central act of the Christian faith, the Communion or Eucharist, takes place.

This celebration recalls how the last night before his death, Jesus celebrated the Passover meal with his friends:

> While they were eating, Jesus took bread, gave thanks and broke it, and gave it to his disciples, saying, "Take and eat; this is my body." Then he took the cup, gave thanks and offered it to them, saying, "Drink from it, all of you. This is my blood of the covenant, which is poured out for many for the forgiveness of sins."
>
> (Matthew 26: 26-8)

People came to the rails to kneel and receive the consecrated Bread and Wine of Communion.

The current wall allows the outline of the original arch to be seen. If there was a medieval roodscreen, an elaborate wooden structure that usually carried a large cross and images of the saints, it is likely to have stood here. At the base of one of the original arches, to the right when facing east, is a carved head, which probably dates to the thirteenth century. This unusual figure, bearded and with luxuriant hair like a layman, looks calmly upwards.

It is close to the larger part of the rare wooden 'triple pulpit' which dominates the small church. At Kilfenora, this is actually a double pulpit with an additional desk on the north side of the altar area. Both of these large reading desks are reached by steps that raise them above the congregation. They are both quite high structures, so the person using them would only have their head and neck visible. Above the south desk, reached by several more stairs, and skirting the carved medieval head, is a higher pulpit.

The clerk read the order of service from the north reading desk, or gave the responses when a more senior official, a clergyman, read them. The clergyman read set portions of the scriptures from the similar desk on the south side. Preaching took place from the higher pulpit. This is a lower structure than the desks, and the clergyman could raise his arms above it to gesticulate as he made his points.

The height is not needed to project the voice in a space so small. It emphasises the breaking open of the Word of God through the sermon. As a theological understanding of preaching, it belongs to the early nineteenth century, and it is probably only the poverty of Kilfenora that enabled these unusual furnishings to survive when Anglican theological trends changed.

Perhaps it was only used when the Dean of Kilfenora preached, or when the bishop visited. One recent bishop, Edward Flewett Darling, used it on Easter Day 1988, but the floor started to collapse beneath him. (*)

A few years earlier, in 1981, Bishop Walton Empey, the Church of Ireland Bishop of Limerick and Killaloe, was installed in this cathedral and a bishop's chair was made

---

* *Newslink* 4, 4, (May 1988) 15.

for the occasion. This is in the Communion area, together with several older chairs.

Around the west end

Leaving the church by its only door, there is a pathway around the west end. Until recently the high cross known as the Doorty Cross stood nearby.

From the outside, the strange form of the west gable end and belfry can be appreciated. A century ago Thomas Westropp gave his view of it. 'Ugly and mean as the little belfry is, it may be mainly ancient and is little worse than that at Corcomroe Abbey. Nothing can excel the ugliness of the west front. Canon Dwyer compares it to a pile of emigrants' luggage with a rabbit-hutch or birdcage overhead.' (*) Its most unusual form has no close parallels in Ireland. It looks uneven because on the north-west corner an attempt was made at some period to build something on, perhaps a buttress to strengthen the west end.

The path passes along the north wall where the indentations caused by later oblong windows inserted in the sixteenth century and later blocked up, can be seen. Also visible is the outline of some of the great stones that form the base of the wall.

The current yellow colour may have been not unlike the original colour, a coating made of local materials mixed with lime to form a render that weatherproofed the building.

In the churchyard there was once a tomb of one Patrick Lysaght who died aged 85 in 1741, according to Westropp after 'a cheerful life, largely dedicated to Mars and

---

* Westropp, "Lisdoonvarna, Kilfenora and Lehinch," 100; Flanagan, *Kilfenora*, 29.

Bacchus' though he adds that he believed he fought bravely on the Continent. (*)

The path leads to the ruined medieval north chapel, which is now covered with a modern clear roof, and houses four of the high crosses.

The side chapel

While the crosses attract immediate attention, it is worth exploring this side-chapel and the rest of the building first. This chapel seems to have been added in the late fifteenth or sixteenth century, and may have been a Lady Chapel, dedicated to the Virgin Mary and used for smaller services and private devotions. The windows emulate the earlier Romanesque and Transitional forms of architecture, in a manner found throughout Ireland at this time. They meld with the style of the older cathedral.

This seems to have been the only medieval addition to the cathedral, and it would have contained one or more of the altars needed in addition to the high altar, to allow the priests attached to the cathedral to say Masses daily.

The west wall has a window with an attractive scalloping around the base of the embrasure. On the opposite wall there is a ruined window and two other long narrow windows of different styles. Between them is a double piscine, used to wash the holy vessels and to drain off the water after the liturgy. This is now very near ground level, and shows how repeated burials have raised the floor level.

A small arch leads off into the chancel or choir, and again reflect show the floor level has risen. This was blocked off in post-Reformation times and later re-opened.

---

* Westropp, "Lisdoonvarna, Kilfenora and Lehinch," 102.

The chancel

The chancel or choir was the part of the cathedral where the associated clergy (or in a medieval monastery the monks) stood to take part in services. Their roles included singing the liturgies of the day.

We can see something of the original cathedral from here, and the fineness of its ornamentation. It was built in what is called Transitional Style, with the new Gothic features, such as pointed arches, blending with the lingering features of Romanesque architecture.

The thirteenth-century east window shows beautiful proportions and is an excellent example of 'School of the West' architecture found this side of the Shannon. It displays features transitional between Romanesque and Gothic. There are three narrow lights, each with a wide embrasure, and they are united by the rolled moulding of a nearly semi-circular arch that ends on one side with a bird pecking, and on the other a floral design. The capitals on each side of the central light include one with foliage and a fluted scallop ornament similar to that of the font inside the church. The other has four clerical heads carved in high relief, all with individual features. They wear cloaks and their hands are joined. Above them is a plain moulding with an egg motif on its upper edge.

Above in the arch, weathering has produced some abstract patterns in the limestone of which the building is made. The high altar once stood beneath this window, the focal point of the church.

I found my desire, yea, I found my desire,
a king rich and generous,
I am a poet seeking graces
as all poets are entitled to demand.

I found strength, yea, I found strength,
a king strong and just,
a king who hearkens to the need of the poor
a king who makes not his laws poorly.

My great king, yea, my great king,
a king who has no interest in wealth.
This is the king who pays each one his due
to all, both little and great.

My own king, yea, my own king,
a king who refuses no one under the sun.
As it is he who pays for my art,
I will praise above all my own king.

Let them be, yea, let them be,
the riches of the host of eternal life.
I shall evermore praise the king of kings,
it is Christ who is best for poetry.

Michael guide, yea, Michael guide,
let me never stray from the path.
I will praise the angel of God
as it is for him alone I found my desire.

***Donnchadh Mór Ó Dálaigh, died 1244.
Trans. MacMurchaidh, Lón Anama:156-7.***

While now open to the sky, Westropp says that there was a belief in 1878 that a hundred years earlier the chancel was still roofed, with an oak ceiling painted blue with gold stars. (*)

On the left of the chancel entrance in the north wall is a fifteenth-century tomb canopy designed like a window, placed, though it is too small, as if it were a sedilia, the seating-place for priests during the liturgy. It has entertaining carvings on it and may have been used at Easter as a focus for the morning Resurrection service. Above it is another head of a bishop wearing a mitre. This is locally regarded as Saint Fachnan. (†)

Below it are gravestones, laid flat. The second from the

* Westropp 1910, 100; and Lisdoonvarna, Kilfenora and Lehinch.
† Westropp, "Lisdoonvarna, Kilfenora and Lehinch", 95, 99.

wall is the oldest with a legible date and is in memory of Hygate Lone, who died in 1638, after being Dean of this church for twenty-one years,.

On the opposite wall, close to where the high altar would have been, is another double piscine for washing the vessels after Communion.

There is a small door in the south side, now with a gate in it, that leads directly to the churchyard. The remains of the 'hanging eye', the round stone which held a round wooden pole on which the door swung, can be seen. There was a similar dent at the bottom. There is also an elegant double lancet window on this side.

A tomb from 1650 now stands attached to the south wall but it seems to originally have been a box-like tomb, and may have been used at some stage as a sepulchre at which the Easter dawn Resurrection service took place. Among the other monuments, it is said that until 1947 the tomb could be seen of Arthur Nihelle, a Catholic bishop of Kilfenora and Kilmacduagh who died in 1795.

On the north wall is a memorial to the wife of Neptune Blood and seven of their children who died young. The family had strong Killinaboy links, and Blood became Dean of Kilfenora. His nephew Thomas Blood lived through, and fought on both sides in, the English Civil War. In 1671 he tried to steal the English Crown Jewels from the Tower of London.

The memorial inscription begins by declaring that humans come forth like flowers and vanish like shadows, as have in silence these beloved children, to the grief of their parents' hearts. The children ranged from a few months old to the godly and thoughtful William who lived to be fifteen.

The high crosses

A particular style of cross is found in early Ireland, at first engraved onto slabs and later in free-standing forms. Many of these free-standing crosses are highly carved, and they may once have been painted as well. Most date from the eighth to tenth centuries. Most of these high crosses contain scenes from the scriptures and sometimes from related apocryphal material. The Kilfenora crosses represent a second period of carving, from the twelfth century. The crosses are of the same size and outline as the earlier ones, but are characterised by having either very little carving on them, or else large figures in high relief. They may have been produced by a distinctive school of carving centred here.

The style of ring-headed cross is believed to derive from the late classical 'Christus victor' design of the crucified but yet triumphant Jesus Christ, surrounded by the laurel wreath of victory. Another suggestion is that the ring-head incorporates a highly stylised form of the Chi-Rho, the first letters of Christ in Greek. The 'R', in Greek a 'P' is imposed centrally upon the 'X' which has been made upright.

St Seanan, east window, external - Photo: B. Meegan

`The follower of God

This poem comes from the twelfth century, but has some verses perhaps as old as the ninth century.

He is pure gold, he is the radiance of the sun,
he is a silver vessel of wine,
he is an angel, he is saints' wisdom
each one who does the will of God.

He is a bird about which closes a snare,
he is a holed ship on the brink of disaster,
he is an empty vessel, a withered tree
each one who does not do the will of God.

He is a fragrant branch in bloom,
he is a vessel filled with honey,
he is a precious stone of fortune
he who does the will of God's heavenly Son.

He is a sinner in whom lies no worth,
he is foul decay, a withered tree,
he is a wild apple branch which blossoms not,
each one who does not do the will of God.

He who does the will of God's heavenly son
is a shining sun in summer,
he is a dais of God in heaven,
he is a vessel of pure crystal.

He is an outstanding steed on a flat plain
the one who strives for the kingdom of the Great God,
He is a chariot which carries the king
and gains victory with golden reins.

He is the sun which warms the hallowed heavens
the one to whom the great king is grateful,
he is a blessed and eminent temple,
he is a holy shrine decorated with gold.

He is an altar from which wine is dispensed
and about which many chants are sung,
he is a pure chalice of wine
adorned with white bronze and gold.

Trans. *MacMurchaidh*, 133-6.

The crosses usually appear to have been placed within the central sacred space of the monastery or at the entrances to the central space. There appear to have been one on each of the four roads into Kilfenora, and others in the central space around the cathedral. There are said to have been originally seven, though only five crosses are now known.

They may have been the focus for private prayer and perhaps also had a role now lost to us in public devotions, possibly similar to that of the later preaching crosses found across medieval Europe.

The crosses seem to have been carved to mark the changes in the Irish church in the twelfth century, and also to mark the establishment of the diocese based at

Kilfenora. The style emphasises the authority of the founder saint as patron and original model for the current bishop. This almost overwhelms the image of Christ crucified and risen.

The Doorty cross

The tall cross in the centre of the display, gets its name from its proximity to the Doorty family grave. During its history, perhaps because it was already broken and lying untended, part of it was used as grave-slab. Later this part was rejoined to the rest of the cross. It was reassembled and re-erected in the 1950s at the west end of the cathedral. In recent years it was brought under cover to protect it from weathering.

The symbolism of the crosses has been lost and any attempts to reconstruct their significance must be tentative. However, the dramatic carving undoubtedly had a considerable significance in its own time.

On the near side is the large figure of a bishop with high conical mitre, or even papal tiara, holding a curved crozier.

The Doorty cross – Photo: R. Power

He is dressed liturgically and is raising his hand in blessing. On each of his shoulders a small winged figure, a bird-like angel with lower legs bare, has alighted. Below him, interlinked, are two smaller but still large figures, who appear to be arm-in-arm, and to have hair or head-coverings. One holds an Old Irish crozier with a simple curve (like a hockey stick), while the other, slighter, figure holds a 'tau' crozier.

A crozier is a staff, modelled on a shepherd's crook, which is the badge of office for both bishop and abbot. As Christ shepherds his 'sheep', his people, and leads them to good pastures, protecting them from the danger of wild animals or thorny thickets, so the bishop or abbot is appointed to protect and guide God's people under Christ. Over the centuries, in different times and places, the crozier developed certain forms. Three of them are seen on this face of the cross.

Turning to the central figures, there are several examples on the older high crosses of scenes depicting the legends of Saints Paul and Anthony meeting in the desert and sharing food brought by a raven. This does not appear to be the main theme here, however, for food, table and bird are absent from this scene.

The figures may have represented the older monastery at Kilfenora ruled by an abbot and with a bishop also present. The intention would then be to demonstrate continuity between the early Christian past and the current order with a bishop appointed from Rome. This bishop superseded the former and took precedence over them. It might also be intended to demonstrate the authority of the see of Saint Peter, and his successor, the pope of the time, over the Irish Church. This would explain why the larger figure, dressed in the up-to-date Roman attire of the twelfth century, is at the top, and in every sense over the two other figures.

A third possibility might be offered, that the slighter of the two linked figures, the one which most clearly has hair or a head-covering, might be female. In this case, there might be a special link with the church at Killinaboy some twelve kilometres to the south on the Ennis road. This site, discussed later, is named after a female saint, Inghean Bhaoith, Innewee, the daughter of Baoith. There was a remarkable 'tau' cross in a similar style of carving on the road between the two sites of Killinaboy and Kilfenora, perhaps at the boundary between the two monastic centres' lands.

Below these two harmonious, linked, figures is a large bird-like figure. It has an open beak and is pecking one of the two human heads below it. The spike of the Irish crozier seems to be holding down the bird and the thrust suggests that it might also hold down the other human head. The heads themselves have no bodies attached but there are arms and hands. One is clutching what seems to be a bag, perhaps containing money, while the hands of the figure who is pecked by the bird, may hold a sword, or possibly a cross.

Various interpretations have been made on why the bird and these two disembodied heads should appear here at the bottom. It has been suggested that they, or the bird, represent evil which the church is subduing. Perhaps it is a reference to the continual small-scale warfare of early Ireland, and perhaps to the associations between battle and birds of carrion, in mythology and reality. Perhaps these are the laity who pay and give, or receive relics, or provide protection for the holy site. Whatever it is, the dynamics of the art mean the eye descends from the top downwards, and these figures are subordinate to the calm upper figures.

The sides of the cross contain further carving, are also decorated with bands of interlace on one side and on the other two large human figures of uncertain meaning. A feature is that many of them have very prominent ears!

The cross may have once had a conical cap, which has been lost.

The other side of the cross displays a large figure of Christ. He is fully robed, with arms open, the Christ depicted in early Christian and Romanesque art, the victor on the morning of the Resurrection as much as the crucified. Like the incised bishop on the tombstone now in the church porch, he appears to be walking, for his feet are pointing in the same direction, and are quite different from the feet of the other figures, which are seen from the front.

There is interlace below in a style associated with Scandinavian design rather than Irish. This is puzzling as this was not an area where the Vikings and their successors had much influence.

Below is a figure on horseback. Below him again appears the shingled roof of a building. This, it has been suggested by the scholar Peter Harbison, represents the pilgrim arriving at the end of his journey, at the shrine of Saint Fachnan.* This pilgrim is wealthy enough to provide a donation to the cathedral, for he has a horse to travel on, but he may represent the many people of all backgrounds who made the journey. However, his feet, both of which can be clearly seen as he sits astride the horse, point in the opposite direction to the feet of Christ above.

The shingled roof may be the roof of a shrine in the Irish style, like a small house, over the tomb believed to be that of Saint Fachnan.

---

* See Harbison, 2000, 2012.

The other cathedral crosses

There is an elegant stone cross, from about the same period, which does not have the distinctive ring-head feature of most Irish high crosses, but gives a similar effect through having carved 'armpits'. It is carved decoratively but has no figures. There are the shafts of two others, both of which have carved decoration but no figures. Neither is nearly as elaborate as the Doorty cross. One of the shafts must be the remains of a particularly fine high cross.

The field cross

Known as the West Cross, this tall cross is accessible over a stile into the field and lies directly opposite the west end of the church, about 200 metres away, on a natural ridge. While seemingly incomplete, it again may have been painted and it has been suggested that other features were associated with it.

The far side of the cross is incised with abstract interlace decoration. The near side has a carving of Christ on the cross. He is fully clothed, in a long-sleeved garment that is pleated below the waist and stretches almost to his feet. The arms are open in embrace rather than at rigid right-angles to his body. His feet rest on a ledge, which might be the top of a very long rope of two strands, or perhaps a long 'tau' crozier. This stretches down the full length of the cross until it merges with rough stonework at the bottom.

It has been suggested by Peter Harbison that a small relic shrine, like the house with a pitched roof found on the Doorty cross, was built against this side of the cross. This would account for the unfinished dressing of the stone where it would have been hidden. If this is the case, the shrine may have held relics of Saint Fachnan.

39

Whether indeed there was a small shrine for relics at the bottom, the arms of Christ seem to be embracing and protecting the sacred centre of the site and its church.

The position of the cross, on the top of the ridge, suggests it was on the edge of the 'sanctissimus', the central holy site of the early Christian monastery, and perhaps in the middle ages it was a final stopping place for pilgrims before they headed for the cathedral to enter.

The Killaloe cross

This may have been the cross which stood on Cross Hill overlooking the site, near the Doctor's Hill road. Like the other Kilfenora crosses, it was only carved in part, but was finely dressed and had the same traditional proportions. It has a solid ring-head, with on one side the figure of Christ, clothed and with arms slightly lower than at right-angles to the body, as if to embrace the onlooker.

It is no longer in Kilfenora. Richard Mant was appointed Bishop of the Church of Ireland United Diocese, based in Killaloe in east Clare, in 1820. He visited Kilfenora that August and described it as 'the worst village I have seen in Ireland as is the most desolate and least interesting country' surrounding it. Perhaps that influenced his thinking with regard to local heritage and personal display. At Killaloe there is an excellent cathedral but no high cross, so Mant acted in a manner not unusual at his time. A letter from the bishop to a friend some years later declares:

> On a visit to Kilfenora in 1820 where there had been five or six stone crosses, I found two or three broken and lying on the ground, neglected and overgrown with weeds. On expressing my concern that these remnants of ecclesiastical antiquity were left in such a state, a clergyman of the parish proposed to send me one of them, which he said could be done

without difficulty or danger of giving offence, as when they were brought to that state the people has no regard for them. One was accordingly sent to Clarisford, and I caused it to be erected among some trees in a picturesque spot, between the house and the canal, having inlaid the shaft with a marble tablet bearing the inscription annexed below. When my daughter was at Clarisford about three years ago, the cross was still standing, being considered I believe, an ornament to the grounds.

After being raised in the grounds of this house near Killaloe, it was moved more than once and apparently blown down in a storm. It was pieced together and came to shelter in 1934, when it was re-erected inside Killaloe cathedral.

The inscription in Latin affixed to the shaft states that the cross collapsed at Kilfenora and had been re-erected at Killaloe by one anxious to preserve church antiquities, by R.M. S.T.P. bishop of both dioceses AD 1821. (*)

Other Kilfenora crosses

High crosses are known to have stood at major entry points to the Kilfenora monastic lands, probably at the entrances already existing in the early Christian embankments. There is a reference by Charles Blake-Foster to a cross standing on a raised mound just to the south of Ballykeal House to the west of Kilfenora, as late as the 1870s, with the head and arms broken off. A small piece was found by John Flanagan built into a wall in 1944. Not far away, a cist grave from about AD 400 was found in 1988. (†)   Westropp refers to a cross in a field wall the north of the church. (‡)

---

* Flanagan, *Kilfenora*, 69-70.
† Flanagan, *Kilfenora*, 72.
‡ Westropp. "Lisdoonvarna, Kilfenora and Lehinch", 104.

There seems to have been a cross on the Corofin road, the R 476, which seems to follow an ancient route from the south. This fell in 1818 and has disappeared, though parts may have been built into local houses. This may have been one of the four which stood at the entrances to what was originally the monastic enclosure, according to George Petrie, who was in charge of the topographical department of the Ordnance Survey from 1833 to 1839.

Another base is now in the grounds of the Catholic church. There may originally have been more crosses, including one each at the entrance to the sacred site. Over the years they may have been lost, or parts used as stones for tombs.

Saint Fachnan's Well

This is to the north-east of the church, and the visitor takes the track that runs from the Visitors' Centre car park behind the east end of the cathedral. This provides an opportunity to see the east window from the outside. There may have been residential buildings, such as a cloister in the area at one time. (*) There are two wells at Bullan, rising out of the limestone, and they may have provided the monastic water-supply in earlier times. The first to be reached was named Toberdane (the first element of which is 'tobar' (meaning 'well'), and had a wall and lintels until about eighty years ago. Saint Fachnan's well is about 300 metres down the track. It is enclosed by a wall on three sides, with an opening to the east, and with limestone lintels covering it. It was repaired in 1687 by the Donald MacDonagh whose tomb is in the church, and a stone at the well commemorates the fact. While there is no regular practice associated with it, at least in recent times, John Flanagan recounts a story that when Saint Fachnan came there was no clear water, so he went

---

* Flanagan, *Kilfenora*, 35.

to Bullan and prayed, which resulted in the current source. (*)

Saint Fachnan's feast day is 14 August, as is the feast of Saint Fachna of Ross Carbery, but in recent times 20 December has been observed.

The older monastery

The cathedral is the focus today. But behind the medieval buildings and the crosses, there is a far older history of Kilfenora, perhaps six centuries of it. None of that original monastery survives, except some outline of the oval form of the dykes and ditches that surrounded the enclosure. The current road system follows these in part.

The original monastic enclosure was a large circular area bounded by a ditch and dyke, the 'termon' or boundary of the monastery. In the central holy space, near where the medieval church now stands, were small buildings, originally of straw and mud, but later of stone. These included small churches, monks' cells or living quarters, a cemetery, and later perhaps high crosses and a round tower (though there is no evidence of one at Kilfenora). One of the small churches may have covered the grave of the founder and served as a shrine dedicated to him. The monastery was under his protection under Christ, and those who worked there and those who died there benefited from his interceding with God for them.

Further away from the centre were other buildings, to house the wider community of workpeople; workshops and storage for foodstuffs.

---

* Flanagan, *Kilfenora*, 21.

To imagine the monastery of the past, or the cathedral of the Middle Ages as it once was, it is necessary to imagine both times of peace with the bustle of travellers seeking lodging, cows lowing, and the sounds of the industry; and the times of warfare, famine or plague that drove people to the shelter of the monastery.

People looked for help during famine, and hospitality when travelling. Often those injured in warfare, or deliberately mutilated in dynastic power-struggles, found refuge here. Many kings and nobles retired to monasteries to spend their last years in prayer and penance, praying for the intercession of the founder saint. Monastic centres were expected to provide spiritual comfort and challenge, healing for illness, and the opportunities to prepare for a good death.

Monasteries were places where the creative arts such as metalwork were practised, and where portable wealth could be kept safely; and where those who lived out their old age there donated wealth for the further upkeep of the monastic community and its role in society.

Monastic rules gave time to prayer and study: and also to labour with the hands and the mind. The copying of the scriptures and other works was part of this labour.

While we have no evidence, Kilfenora was ideally situated for the production of books. Two of the main materials were easily available, the skins of new-born calves from which to make the vellum on which to write; and the nearby Burren's limestone to burn to make the lime baths necessary for its production. In later times Kilfenora was known as the place where the cattle came down from the Burren in spring when they were in calf. Fairs were held, and this may have been the case in earlier times too. Sheep and goats were also grazed on the Burren, and the skins of lamb and kid were also used for making

> Pleasant to me is the glittering of the sun today upon these margins, because it flickers so.
>
> *Irish, ninth century marginal note. Trans. Jackson, 177.*
>
> My hand is weary with writing
> My sharp quill is not steady,
> My slender-beaked pen jets forth
> A black draught of shining dark-blue ink.
>
> A stream of wisdom of blessed God
> Springs from my fair-brown shapely hand:
> On the page it squirts its draught
> Of ink of the green-skinned holly.
>
> My little dripping pen travels
> Across the plain of shining books,
> Without ceasing for the wealth of the great –
> Whence my hand is weary with writing.
>
> *Irish, twelfth century, trans Meyer, Selections, 89.*

parchment for writing. As with cattle, the skins of the new-born were preferred.

It seems possible, if we compare it with the Pictish monastery of Portmahomack, which was destroyed by fire in about the year 800, that all the work of slaying calves, preparing vellum and writing all happened on one site. There are no records to say that this actually happened here, but the materials were available.

If this community ever did the same as many other monasteries and wrote the *Life* of their own founder saint, Fachnan, it has long been lost.

The medieval period

One of the intriguing aspects of Kilfenora is that it was clearly a site of major significance in the Middle Ages, but we are not entirely sure why. In ancient times there was a major royal site and centre of political power nearby. It was important enough in the twelfth century to be chosen as a bishop's site, and had enough money, at least for a time, to build an imposing cathedral with fine carvings and presumably similar high-quality furnishings.

There are few records in the Irish Annals, the year-by-year list of events which forms the backbone for early Irish historical research. There is also a dearth of the other kinds of medieval records we might expect, concerning appointments, land ownership and similar matters. It seems, though, that from time to time the cathedral was in financial difficulties. Even the school of sculpture, which appears to have been based here, had only relatively local impact.

The bishops traced themselves back spiritually to Saint Fachnan, and like most early Christian monasteries there was probably a local bishop attached to the monastic centre, up to the twelfth century. They are also called Bishops of Corcomroe, and are poorly recorded. As Ireland became more in line with European practice, bishops became fewer in number and had a more clearly marked geographical territory within an archdiocese. In the case of Kilfenora, the archdiocese was Cashel.

It is the smallest diocese in Ireland, thirty-seven kilometres long and eighteen wide; and lies entirely within County Clare

There is a list of the medieval and later bishops in the *Ordnance Survey Letters* of John O'Donovan from 1839. A colourful if inaccurate *Annals of Kilfenora* was published in the nineteenth century by the antiquarian Charles Blake-Foster. The list is repeated by Westropp (*), and further details of the bishops, especially the Catholic incumbents, are recounted by John Flanagan.

Local rulers and later the O'Brien lords, who at various times had established the cathedrals of Killaloe and Saint

---

* Westropp, "Lisdoonvarna, Kilfenora and Lehinch", 105-7.

Mary's, Limerick, were significant patrons in earlier times. The family would have used the church, and members were among the leading clergy. Among them in the fourteenth century was a dean, Maurice O'Brien, who was buried in Limerick.

Of the medieval bishops, whether native Irish or incoming Normans, we know very little. An unnamed bishop swore an oath of fealty to King Henry II in 1172, in the early years of the Anglo-Norman presence in Ireland, which had a further powerful impact on the Irish church. Other bishops are mentioned by first name in the course of the thirteenth century. Kilfenora covered what were later the baronies of the Burren and Corcomroe, but this was still a small diocese, in spite of its impressive cathedral.

During the Middle Ages, it is likely that there was a community of secular canons living nearby, probably living to the Augustinian rule, and fulfilling the cathedral's religious functions as their forerunners had done. There is no sign of a cloister, the domestic buildings usually found on the south side of a monastic church, but there is the slight local tradition that there were buildings to the east of the cathedral, not far from Saint Fachnan's well. The priests who took the services, and saw to the spiritual and perhaps physical needs of the pilgrims, would certainly have lived somewhere nearby, even if we are not sure exactly where.

Later times

The form of worship changed as a consequence of the Reformation, though it is uncertain which tradition dominated at different times, for it is possible that possession of the cathedral church changed hands more than once.

After the Reformation the canons would have been replaced by secular Anglican clergy. There are two lines of bishops, though it is not clear when the first Protestant bishop was appointed. There are references to a mid-sixteenth-century John, a preacher who was buried here, who may have administered the cathedral.

One Bernard Adams made a Return to the Royal Commissioners in 1615, saying that there were ten canon's portions belonging to Kilfenora cathedral, each to the value of fourteen shillings. In ten years of residence he had been unable ever to claim the five marks rent due from the Aran Islands. In 1628 King Charles I nominated a bishop, who visited but declined acceptance when he saw the poverty of the See. (*)

During the eighteenth and nineteenth centuries the Church of Ireland had a Dean resident, which retained the standing of the church as a cathedral. Kilfenora was in fact an independent Church of Ireland diocese until 1752. The last bishop of Kilfenora was John Whitcombe, (1742-1752). It was then united in stages into what is now the Church of Ireland diocese of Limerick, Killaloe, Ardfert, Aghadoe, Kilfenora, Clonfert, Kilmacduagh and Emly.

In 1837 the diocese of Kilfenora contained nineteen parishes, formed into six unions; there were only three parish churches and one other place in which services took place

In the nineteenth century, the Church of Ireland Dean of Kilfenora lived at Ballybreen House off the R 481 Ennistymon Road. Now a ruin, it is thought that some of the stones for the house and farm buildings may have come from a much earlier stone fort. Nearby is a limestone slab in a field which is carved with a human

---

* See Swinfen, *Kilfenora* 6-7.

hand. It is said to be pointing to where the altar vessels were hidden by Catholics in Penal Times, the period when legislation existed to prevent Catholic worship.

In Catholic terms, since the nineteenth century the diocesan area has been administered by the Diocese of Galway. It was united first with Kilmacduagh and then both were united with Galway in 1883. For technical reasons the decision was a papal one, which has led to the common belief that the Pope is the Bishop of Kilfenora.

There were certainly times of religious hostility but also periods when relations may have been more cordial. It is possible that at later times the choir and nave of the cathedral were used by Catholics and Anglicans respectively. As a scheduled ancient monument it is now in the care of the State, though the nave remains a Church of Ireland church.

While we can only speculate on how people lived in the past, the area round Kilfenora has been regarded as fertile agricultural land on the edge of the Burren, and has a local river supplying water. For centuries it was the place of great livestock fairs, especially of cattle. The town was already in decline by 1837 and this continued as nearby Ennistymon grew. However, there were fairs on 04 June, 15 August (the Catholic feast of the Assumption of the Virgin Mary and the day after Saint Fachnan's feast day) and 09 October; and in summer a weekly butter-market. The opening of the West Clare railway at Ennistymon in 1887 signalled the continuing decline, and though a branch line to Kilfenora was proposed it was not built. Animals were taken elsewhere for transport and Kilfenora dwindled to the small town it is today.

By 1942-3 there were about one hundred residents in Kilfenora, but it remained an important village for cattle and sheep fairs. A Tourist Association report for this period reflects the seasonal influxes into the village, for there were seven public houses, about ten groceries, a Post Office, a Guards' Barracks, a National School, a sports' field a kilometre away, and a Catholic church. (*)

Services in the cathedral were reported as no longer, though they later revived for a time.

Lingering in Kilfenora

Kilfenora is a good place to start local walks. There is a hostel and a number of bed and breakfast places. Bars provide meals, and socially the small town is known for its music, in impromptu sessions. The Kilfenora Ceili Band is now over one hundred years old. A number of local groups, one of which is a Farmers' Co-operative (*http://www.farmheritagetours.com*) enable people to explore the landscape and the smaller, lesser-known monuments.

The Burren Centre is run by a local Co-operative and has a film display of the history of the Burren from ancient times. The website, http://www.kilfenoraclare.com, gives details of local accommodation and events.

---

* I.T.A Survey 1942/3.

Holy wells

Many wells in Ireland have been associated with reverence for a particular saint.

In the past a good stream of pure water was vital for the local community and their livestock, and some wells had both a devotional role and a practical one.

Wells associated with cures for eyes are particularly common. Traditional houses often had no chimney or smoke-vent and smoke from the hearth fire lingered under the thatch, causing irritation to the eyes.

Many holy wells had local 'patterns', prayers undertaken, usually as an individual act, which involved walking in a set circle, saying certain prayers at stopping places, in a set form. The pilgrim also drank of the water, or applied it to the eyes, and often left a small votive offering. The saint's Pattern Day, Patronal or feast day, held particular significance, and in the past large numbers of people would undertake the devotional round of prayers on this day. Often celebrations of a more secular nature followed.

Sometimes items are left at a holy well, or on a nearby tree. These can be something associated with the person prayed for, or prayer cards and similar small items. These are left untouched.

A number of holy wells have been restored in recent times, and some are signposted.

Mar tobar glé trí croí na lice
Bruchtann an dóchas trí chroí an dhuine.

Like a clear spring through the heart of a stone
Hope breaks out through the human heart.

Traditional proverb

There are a huge number of sites in the area, which serve to show the importance of this area at the foot of the Burren, from the time of the first inhabitants onwards.

One of the richest roads to walk is the one to Noughaval, taking the R.476 where it turns off the main street at Linnane's Bar, signed for Lisdoonvarna; and then taking the second road to the right after a few hundred metres.

The historic fort of Ballykinvaraga, Cathair bhaile cinn Mhargaidh, 'locally pronounced Ballykinwarraga' according to O'Donovan in the *Ordnance Survey Letters*, is about two kilometres along this road to the left. This site dates from about 200 B.C. and means the Fort of the Chief Market, a place of local significance, community gathering and secular power to which the development of Kilfenora must be related. The fort is constructed of large blocks of stone, and has substantial ramparts. The gate is to the south-east and a sunken passage leads through an unusual Chevaux de Frise. This 'Frozen horsemen' defence is created by placing upright stones unevenly for some metres outside the walls. Some medieval coins were found near the gateway, which suggests it continued as an assembly place, as did other places with similar names in Ireland.

Near this road are numerous other sites, including Saint Caimín's well, which in local tradition was good for curing eyes. John Flanagan tells a story of how a Kilfenora woman with a blind daughter prayed for her there, while the child fell asleep, and awoke cured. (*)

The road leads to Noughaval, the 'new settlement', which may have been one of the churches in close association with the cathedral; and was later one of its parishes. Like several of the associated churches, it may have had a round tower. Some large stones now lying at the entrance

---

* Flanagan, *Kilfenora*, 22.

to the churchyard on the left appear to have been dressed for a circular structure. The churchyard has a cross set upright in a slab in the churchyard similar to that found on some of the pilgrim 'stations' on the Burren. The stone may have been used as a Mass-rock, an open-air altar used by Catholics during Penal Times.

There is also a rare market cross at the entrance to the churchyard. The current Catholic Church is a former Church of Ireland building which was bought, moved from Ballyvaughan, and rebuilt here in the 1940s. There is a holy well nearby.

Continuing on this road brings the walker on to the R 480 near Caherconnell stone fort, and then to Poulnabrone portal tomb, a distance of about ten kilometres.

Alternatively, by crossing the R480, the road passes up the Burren to Carron, where there is a fine twelfth century church and holy well dedicated to Saint Cronan; and a series of later stations associated with the local Saint Fachnan's well.

An alternative walk is the one outlined below in Section Two, which follows the medieval route back to Dysert O'Dea in the south, using small local roads that avoid the ancient route, the now busy and narrow R 476 towards Ennis.

Grazing on the Burren

The high limestone area of North Clare known as the Burren (An Bóireann, 'the great rock'), has a unique landscape and has been farmed for millennia. Early farmers in the days before iron implements found the light soils easier to work than the heavier soils that cover much of Ireland. We can see a great deal of pre-historic and historic remains, especially tombs. Something that touches all periods of history is preserved in the remarkable stone walls. Some are ancient and relatively recent: their origins can be surmised through the height of the rock pedestals preserved beneath the different styles of stone. There are also the 'green roads', un-surfaced routes, some of which may be very ancient indeed.

During the last Ice Age, fingers of ice swept over the area, gouging the land down to the bare rock in some places, and carving it into the forms we see. In between, valleys were left where plants and wildlife survived. The area is one of outstanding beauty and rare plants flourish, some of them relatives of European alpine species, and some related to the plants of the Arctic tundra.

The Burren is also a place of unusual agricultural practice. In Ireland as in many grazing societies, the practice of transhumance, moving animals to different lands in winter and summer, was followed. On the Burren, contrary to usual practice, the animals went on to the high land in winter and came down for the summer.

The limestone nature of the Burren means that it absorbed summer heat and released it slowly, making it relatively warm for the animals in the winter. Further, there was surface water available but not the surfeit found in the boggy lowlands. Moving stock down in summer to the lush grasses of the lowlands left behind lands which had benefited from grazing, and where the natural hazel had been prevented from choking out other plant-life.

Not all breeds of cattle can manage the alkaline-rich lands of the Burren, but local breeds have adapted and until relatively recently farmers with grazing rights might walk their cattle from twenty miles away to make use of these lands. The cattle themselves have remained remarkably sure-footed. There has been less sheep-grazing on the Burren in recent times, but feral goats can be found. Their ancestors are thought to have been once domesticated but have long since run wild. Some of the current genetic heritage may go back to prehistoric times, and they continue to contribute to the ecological balance of the locality

KILLINABOY
and south to the estuary

THE first part of this route, to Killinaboy, is just over twelve kilometres long, only three kilometres longer than the main road.

Leaving Kilfenora by the Doctor's Hill road, at the corner with the Máire Rua shop, the first hill on the left is Cross Hill, where a high cross stood over the monastic centre.

After 2.6 kilometres, a crossroads is reached (signed right for Lakeside Lodge). Taking the left turning, there is an old burial ground on the right after a further 2.3 kilometres. After a further 2.8 kilometres there is a T-junction and the walker turns right here. There is a marshy area on the right. The suggested route turns left after 900 metres at the crossroads, stays on this road for another four kilometres (passing a megalithic tomb on the left, evidence of the long settlement in this landscape), then takes a left turn marked Burren Way, the L5248. This crosses the Fergus again and after another kilometre rejoins the main R476.

This road gives a chance to gain a sense of the scenery below the Burren and the kind of plant and wild-life of this limestone landscape. There are views of the stratified limestone formation of the Burren itself, including the tilted sides of Mullaghmore.

A number of the houses along the road are single-storey buildings with a gable-end that faces into the wind, a style that is based on older vernacular dwellings. The turf was traditionally stacked against the far gable-end, allowing it to keep as dry as possible before being brought inside for use. Turf was taken from the lowlands, by farmers who had bog rights, or was sold by those who had.

The traditional style of building in this area was of limestone blocks, covered inside and out with a lime mortar. Thatch was used extensively for roofing, made of rushes from local river-beds. Slate was also used, while Liscannor flagstone roofs are also common, and unique to North Clare. Also used since the late nineteenth century is corrugated iron, which is now regarded as a traditional roofing material.

Much of this walk follows the River Fergus, on which Ennis is situated and which drains into the Shannon through a large estuary. The river was used for transport since the time of early travellers. Shortly before the road, the L5248, turns left and crosses the Fergus, the river has gone underground through a swallow-hole for a kilometre before re-emerging. There is also a cave nearby which deposits water that has travelled underground from the turlough (temporary lake created when there is a surfeit of water underground) at Carran on the Burren, some eight kilometres distant. The hydrology of the area is still only partially understood.

At this point the road meets the R 476 again. Turning right onto it, there is a turn left after 100 metres, on to the L3096 (marked Burren Way), and a diversion of a few kilometres takes the walker onto the limestone plateau, with Parknabinna, a megalithic wedge tomb, at the top. Another such tomb, a little further along, was recorded in *Griffith's Valuation*, shortly after the Great Famine, as being the home of a widow and her young son.

Alternatively (though unsuited to walkers as the R476 is both busy and narrow), at the junction with the R 476, turning left back 1.1 kilometres reaches the place where the 'tau cross' stood on Roughan Hill, and where a replica stands today. This is on the left of the road, in a small clump of trees, just before the L5260 turn on the left. The actual cross is in Corofin Heritage Centre. John O'Donovan suggested that the name Roughan is a family name and the townland (local civil land division) was Baile Uí Reabhacháin (or Robhacháin). There was a church family of this name mentioned in the Annals. If they held these lands from the church, this might be a reason why the 'tau' cross stood here.

Just before, there is on the same side the site of a hill-fort with a souterrain, an underground passage area possibly used to store and cool foodstuffs such as dairy products.

To remain on the route to Killinaboy, however, the walker turns right from the L5248, along the R476 for 700 metres, to reach the distinctive church at Killinaboy.

Killinaboy

This church and monastic site in a bend of the River Fergus, is Cill, the church, of Inghean Bhaoith, the daughter of Baoith. Like several early Irish saints, she is known by her father's name rather than her own. Nothing is known about her directly, even whether she ever existed. The name may be pre-Christian, or may be a figurehead for women of a tribe of Baoith who followed the religious life.

It is one of the few sites to have a female patron, and whatever the origin, she is an important local figure, with several holy wells dedicated to her. In later accounts of the saints she figures as the mother, or aunt, of Saint Senan of Scattery Island. She is also credited (perhaps in a spiritual rather than physical sense) with having forty-five, or fifty-six, children, many of whom were saints. She is elsewhere named as the aunt of Saint Brigit of Kildare. Her own name has been given in later sources as Fíónmhaith, 'wine-good', 'good like wine'; or Cuman, which the writer understood to mean 'favour'.

Gable with two-armed cross
- Photo: R. Power

Sometimes Fionnmhaith, meaning both 'blond', and 'of good virtue', is taken to be the name. The English from 'Innewee' was once a popular name for girls, but John O'Donovan noted that its use was in decline by the time he visited in 1839.

There are the remains of an early Christian circular enclosure in some of the surrounding fields, and the monastic settlement was clearly substantial. Although dedicated to a female saint, there is nothing that might indicate it was a women's foundation. The modern road cuts through the settlement and the older churchyard at a sharp angle. The ruined church was rebuilt extensively in the later middle ages, when it was a parish church.

The round tower, of which there is only a stump left, may have been raised in the twelfth century, perhaps earlier. It was probably originally about 20 metres high. As the church site stands on a natural rocky outcrop, it is likely to have been visible for miles above the tree-cover of medieval Ireland. It would have been a marker for those travelling to the foot of the Burren, a sign for travellers seeking hospitality. It is thought to have been damaged in the seventeenth-century Cromwellian Wars. The prominence of the site, and perhaps its wealth and significance, meant that Killinaboy received other attention as well down the centuries.

In 1599 the *Annals of the Four Masters* note that 'O'Donnell remained that night encamped at Cill-Inghine-Baoith, and left it before noon on the following day; and he then proceeded to Kilfenora in the cantred of Corcomroe'. He used Kilfenora as a base for his raiding parties, and returned northwards, avoiding the monastery of Corcomroe.

Unusually, the tower here is some way to the north of the church, rather than in the usual position near the north side of the west gable. Why the stone church was not built in the usual alignment is unknown: perhaps there was some shrine, or the ground was considered unsuitable.

Round towers

A round tower, *cloigtheach* in Irish, literally bell-tower, is a native form of building found on Irish monastic sites. There are the remains of, or written reports of, about a hundred, while a further two can be found in Scotland and one on the Isle of Man. They were constructed between the ninth and twelfth centuries, during the Viking period and afterwards, some possibly as late as the twelfth-century Reform of the Irish Church. The dimensions of circumferences to height are the same, and they taper upwards, giving a graceful outline.

Construction must have been a major undertaking, requiring skilled workmen. They needed timber scaffolding, probably both internal and external; and stone which was hewn, transported and dressed to the curve of the building,

Most are constructed on a stone plinth and with little other evidence of foundations, though it is possible that some had an internal foundation of rubble below the level of the doorway. Apart from two (one of them on Scattery Island), the door is some way above the ground, meaning that access was by an external and perhaps moveable wooden ladder. It is usually on the south side.

Within the tower there were several floors of made of wood, which were accessed by ladders. There is usually a window to give light to each storey, and four windows at the top. A bell could be rung from here, for the hours of prayer and other services. It was presumably a large and heavy hand-bell, similar to those preserved as relics of early Christian saints, and would have been kept on the upper floor.

Some round towers have decoration over doors or windows but are generally unadorned. They were presumably places of storage, perhaps of foodstuffs and of precious items, both those belonging to the monastery and those deposited there for safe-keeping. They may also have been used on feast-days for the display of certain relics, from the door above the ground, which would have allowed more people to see them.

They also seem to have become symbols, and references to towers of prayer rising from monasteries towards the heavens may be derived from them. Another use was as way-markers for pilgrims.

As places of refuge they were of little use. To an antagonist, Norseman or native, they were an attractive chimney. We know that some suffered from fire, with the contents, and occupants, destroyed.

The original church seems to have been twelfth- or early thirteenth-century, and some of the stones in the north wall are of the huge kind associated with that period, or even earlier times. The original door might well have been in the traditional style, a trabeate doorway at the west end, with a stone lintel and slight slope to the doorway. A slightly curved line of masonry in the west wall still exists. The door was moved, perhaps as late as the fifteenth century, to the south side, but there remains on the outer side of the west gable, above this line, a large stone two-armed cross.

The original road may have led across the fields from the west, so pilgrims would have seen this cross, in relief and perhaps covered with white plaster, marking the arrival at a major place of prayer. This style of cross is associated with the Holy Sepulchre in Jerusalem, and often known as the patriarchal cross. It may be that Killinaboy once held a relic known to have been in County Clare and thought to be part of the 'true cross', the cross on which Jesus was crucified. This was believed to have been found by Saint Helena, mother of the Emperor Constantine, in the early fourth century, and the finding prompted the emperor to build the church of the Holy Sepulchre in Jerusalem.

The cross, which is out of alignment with the current gable-ends, may have been part of the original church. A sign of this building is the 'ante' in the north wall, stonework that juts out horizontally, a feature of earlier Irish stone churches that copies the style of older timber churches. When the south side of the gable was rebuilt, the ante was copied on this side too.

Jerusalem was the physical place of the Jewish temple and then Jesus' Resurrection. As well as being the chief focus of Christian pilgrimage, it had a symbolic value. More, the monastic life was based around the daily recitation of the 150 Psalms. Many of these are pilgrimage songs, speaking of the journey to, and arrival at, the temple in Jerusalem.

Psalm 84

How lovely is your dwelling place, Lord, God of hosts.
My soul is longing and yearning,
is yearning for the courts of the Lord.
My heart and soul ring out their joy
to God, the living God.

The sparrow herself finds a home
and the swallow a nest for her brood;
she lays her young by your altars,
Lord of hosts, my king and my God.

They are happy who dwell in your house,
forever singing your praise.
They are happy whose strength is in you,
in whose hearts are the roads to Zion.

As they go through the bitter valley
they make it a place of springs
[the autumn rain covers it with blessings],
they walk with ever growing strength,
they will see the God of Gods in Zion.

O, Lord God of hosts, hear my prayer,
give ear, O God of Jacob.
Turn your eyes, O God, our shield,
look on the face of your anointed.

One day within your courts
Is better than a thousand elsewhere.
The threshold of the house of God
I prefer to the dwellings of the wicked.

For the Lord God is a rampart, a shield;
he will give us favour and glory.
The Lord will not refuse any good
to those who walk without blame.

Lord, God of hosts,
happy the one who trusts in you.

The much-rebuilt church is interesting for other features. Above the door is a large Sheila-na-gig. Inside we have evidence of some later adaptations, perhaps a statue niche to the left as we face where the altar once stood, similar to a niche or cupboard of similar size and age at the fifteenth-century church at Kilraghtis near Barefield, north of Ennis. The windows are similar to those at Lemanagh castle. The church was repaired in 1715 and continued in use. John O'Donovan notes that the church was rebuilt by Catholics in 1725, when it was originally thatched. The low door in the north wall could have led to a vestry (the floor-level has risen), and the medieval canopied tomb had been reused by the 1890s. The many tombstones inside and outside the church show how much it remained in use locally, while standing and when in ruins.

The Killinaboy lands may have extended to the north as far as the site of the 'tau' cross on Roughan Hill, which would make this carving a boundary marker.

A worn medieval slab shaped like a tombstone lies in the corner of the churchyard south-west of the doorway. It is carved with a long thin 'tau cross', that ends in a wider bell or house-shaped form. Perhaps this represented an abbatical cross, above a reliquary or a bell. It may have been like the small bell of similar shape associated with Saint Cuana which was revered around Kilshanny further west in Clare and is now in the British Museum.

Whether the stone stood upright, and whether it was specifically in honour of Inghean Bhaoith as founder and patron, it is impossible to say. Like many sites on this route, historical records are sparse, though this saint was much honoured.

In the vicinity is a holy well on the R476, dedicated to Innewee, Inghean Bhaoith, whose feast day was 29 December. The waters were said to be healing for sore eyes. There are other wells close to the church, and also the ruins of a Famine village, a group of homes that were deserted in the course of Ireland's Great Famine of 1845-49.

Other places in County Clare also contain dedications to Inghean Bhaoith, such as the three wells in Kilnamona parish further west.

A social anthropological study was made in the 1930s in the Killinaboy area and published in 1940 as *Family and Community in Ireland.*

One of the holy wells lies nearby but on a dangerous bend. As the R476 is not advisable for walkers, it is suggested following it for 400 metres and then turning right on to the L5250. A further two kilometres takes the walker to Crossard.

Crossard

The ruined wall on the right by the T-junction is the remains of a Moravian Church built in 1794. Moravians trace their origins back to the late medieval reformer Jan Hus, who was executed in Prague in 1415. Moravian theology was summed up during the seventeenth-century by the bishop John Comenius, who lived at the time of the Thirty Years War of religion: In things essential - unity; in non-essentials - liberty; in all things – charity. There remains no higher term of address in the Moravian Church than Brother or Sister.

After war and persecution the survivors regrouped in the early eighteenth in what is now eastern Germany. Moravians also settled in London, developing a base for missions to the slaves in the Caribbean, to Greenland and elsewhere. They influenced the young John Wesley, and it was with them that he had the religious experience that shaped the remainder of his life and the founding of the Methodist societies.

> If we cannot as yet think alike in all things, at least we may love alike. Herein we cannot possibly do amiss. For of one point none can doubt a moment: God is love; and he that dwelleth in love, dwelleth in God, and God in him...So far as we can, let us always rejoice to strengthen each other's hands in God.
> **John Wesley, Letter to a Roman Catholic, 1749**

The Moravians at Crossard gathered in the later eighteenth century, under the influence of the Burton family, owners of Clifton House beside Inchiquin

Lough. The church was not open for long, though it was the scene of fairly substantial congregations for a time. During the 1798 Rising, the Burtons fled to Limerick for safety and numbers dwindled. It was served for a time by visiting ministers, and was then used as a hedge-school. It is recorded as having some 220 pupils in 1826.

The ministers' manse, also ruined, is the other side of the road. It became the parish priest's house until destroyed in an accidental fire in 1827.

Nearby is the earlier eighteenth-century Poplar House, which was occupied by the Burtons until Clifton House was completed. It once had a basement, and local stories give it a Catholic background, that priests said Mass secretly here during Penal times, and could escape if needed through a secret tunnel.

The road to the left comes down the side of Inchiquin Lough, with views over the water. The ruins on the northern shore today are those of a fifteenth-century tower-house, a replacement for an earlier O'Brien castle on a wooded island in the lake. Some of the minor roads are thought to be old booleying paths, used for moving cattle to seasonal pastures.

Further down the road on the left is Clifton House. At its entry, beside the river stands another O'Brien tower-house, which dates from the fifteenth century, and later had a fortified house attached. Staying on the road to the T-junction and then turning left for another two kilometres brings the walker back to the outskirts of Corofin, meeting the main road at the grotto.

Corofin

This is a late settlement in its present form, with the Church of Ireland Saint Catherine's built between 1715 and 1720, though it is possibly on an earlier church site.

The church, on the R460 towards Gort, is now the Heritage Centre and houses the 'tau' cross which originally stood on Roughan Hill.

This is a solid carved structure, which is thought to have been much higher in the past when the shaft was longer. There are two human heads with serene features at each of the upper ends. They are without beards and each has a head-covering and a long neck. They are banded together in the centre by three carved folds. This rare cross is thought from the carving to date to the twelfth century.

The 'tau', the Greek letter 'T', is the shape of the early Irish crozier, so it has monastic connections. Its early symbolic use relates to the story of the meeting of Saints Paul and Anthony, two of the Desert Fathers. Like the Old Testament prophet Elijah, they were fed by a raven in the desert. This became a reference to the Eucharist, as well as to monastic harmony. While the raven is not shown on this tau cross, the idea would have been in people's minds.

While religious relationships were often tolerant in this area, a noted exception came in the early nineteenth century. Edward Synge, a proselytising landlord, became the subject of a bitter dispute. In 1831 he was shot at, and his servant, a man named Donnellan, was killed. Synge was saved because a bullet aimed at him lodged in the bible which he carried in his breast pocket. The incidents were blamed on the 'Terry Alts', a secret agrarian society of the time. The bible is on display in the Centre.

There is also a poignant exhibition of famine and other local material from an area that was badly affected in the 1840s, and where many starved or died of illness.

On permanent display are copies of the works of the nineteenth-century local artist Frederick William Burton (1816-1900) from Clifton House, who became curator of the National Gallery in London.

The Catholic church close by has fixed to its outer wall the stone head of a bishop taken from Rath.

There is a nineteenth-century bridge across the Fergus. Walkers will find food, accommodation (including a hostel) and entertainment in the village.

The route follows the R476 over the bridge and then after some 100 metres, taking a turn right onto the R460 signed for Inagh (and Ennistymon). After about a kilometre the old West Clare railway station, now a private house, can be seen. Taking the next road left to cross the Fergus and then immediately right again brings the walker towards Rath. After a further two kilometres there is a signed turn right, and it lies a further two kilometres along this road. (The sign also identifies Rath as a stopping place on the Dysert O'Dea History Trail.)

Rath

This beautiful site, often known as Rath Blathmach (Ráith Bhlathmhaic), the fort, or settlement of Blathmac (later spelt Blathmach) is on a hilltop and looks over the small Lough Raha and a ruined tower-house on its shore. There are views of the high Burren, especially the tilted, stepped mountain known as Mullaghmore. The site is dedicated to an eighth-century saint Blathmac, whose name contains the element 'blath', flower. He is believed to have founded a small monastic settlement here.

There is another Blathmac known from the eighth century, who wrote a long poem addressed to the Virgin Mary, recounting episodes from her life and mourning with her the death of Jesus. This poem was to be said at night as an aid to devotion:

Noble is the being who has been born to you! There has been granted to you, Mary, a great gift; Christ, son of God, the Father in Heaven, him you have borne in Bethlehem.

It was manifest, maiden, when you were with your son in Bethlehem of Juda: an angel of bright fame announces his birth to the shepherds.

A star of great size was seen, which Balaam, son of Beoir, had prophesied; it was it that guided from the east the three magi bearing gifts. .....

Then they found your son with you, dear Mary; the three magi that I mention offered fine gifts.

These, then were the gifts, gold, frankincense and myrrh; all this was fitting for Jesus, a king who was God, who was true man.

An angel of God from Heaven showed another way to the magi. They did not go to Herod – they went safe to their own land.

Carney, Blathmac, stanzas 10-18, pp. 4-7

Late sources, which often connect saints in this way, make him one of the numerous children of Inghean Bhaoith of Killinaboy, and therefore a relative of Saint Senan of Scattery Island, who is variously called her son or her nephew. Blathmach is named in another poem associated with Senan as one of the saints who can be appealed to should Scattery suffer any wrong. (*) Other sources include his role as mentor to other Clare saints, including Flannan of Killaloe.

---

* Plummer, *Miracles of Senan*, 29.

As with Fachtnan and Inghean Bhaoith, there was no *Life* of this saint, and his legacy is mainly in the continuing use of this site. A crozier associated with him is now in the National Museum, as are two early Irish bronze bells which were kept here until the nineteenth century.

While the sound from the bells used by early Irish Christians do not seem to have travelled far, especially when there was no water close by to magnify it, it would have been heard in the settlement, and perhaps below it, to the edge of the surrounding forests and to the lough.

There seems to have been a round tower here, the remains of which were taken down in 1838. Some of the stones in the wall enclosing the churchyard may have belonged to it as they appear dressed for a round building. As Dysert O'Dea is only two kilometres away, and also has a tower, they must have both been easily visible to people in the area, and indeed perhaps in competition. This may have continued down the years: Westropp in the late nineteenth century refers to: 'the absurd popular legend of the removal of Dysert Tower from Rath'.

This wall also has a bullaun stone built into it upside-down in the corner to the right as the site is entered. These stones, with small circular hollows in them, sometimes more than one, are often found at early church sites, though their original use is uncertain.

The church is late medieval, but was rebuilt from at least one earlier stone church, and the huge stones at the base of the remaining walls are probable signs of a twelfth-century church. Peter Harbison suggested that this site was an alternative starting point for the twelfth century pilgrimage route to Kilfenora that he proposes; and that this and other churches like the one at Killinaboy were

Sheela-na-gigs

At Killinaboy, Rath and some other places in County Clare, can be found sexually-explicit carvings of naked women known as sheela-na-gigs. There are about a hundred in Ireland, and others in Britain and to a lesser extent in France. Most have no hair, bulging eyes, and an aggressive pose, with a contorted figure, and enlarged sexual organs. Sheela-na-gigs are found mainly on churches and the later tower-houses, and are often at gable-ends or near doors and windows. While there have been several attempts to interpret them since the mid-nineteenth-century, the most likely explanation is that they are examples of apotropaic magic, magic to frighten away enemies. Their association with churches may suggest that the main enemies are evil spirits, and that they ward them off from these centres of religious practice and community gathering.

rebuilt in the fifteenth century during a revival of the pilgrimage.

The ruins contain remains of fine carvings, while fragments of carved stone can be found marking graves or built into the surrounding wall. There is a medieval holy water stoup beside the door on the south side.

Exceptionally beautiful is the remains of the window frame inset on the south wall. This is from about the year 1200. It was originally for an outer window and this part has been replaced in the wall upside-down. A central, but rather friendly monster has large ears with a ring design on them. These are being licked by two snakes with teeth (visible in 1891 when Westropp visited), with their bodies forming the inner mouldings of the window. The outer moulding also ends in two twisted beasts' heads just under the central monster's head. In between is carved foliage. Other carvings include a small sheela-na-gig. Its head is, like the monster's, between two beasts that seem to be licking its ears.

The sill of the later window on the south wall is also finely carved, and seems to have been reused in this position.

Nature poetry

Early Irish nature poetry may derive from traditions pre-dating the arrival of Christianity. They are a native response to the Psalms, with their nature poetry; to the world in which the writers lived; and perhaps to the poetic traditions already current in Ireland.

Most of the aspects of nature praised in the poems and prayers give delight in their own right, but they also speak of how the world provides food or shelter, for humans or for their livestock.

Nature can be harsh – snow, frost and ice silence the land and prevent humans travelling, while wolves howl and birds droop with cold - but there is also a great deal of pleasure taken in the natural world, and in the life of prayer adopted by the writers.

The following poem is almost making affectionate fun of the hermit lifestyle. It is attributed to Suibhne, a king who, cursed by a saint, went mad in battle and lived wild ever after.

> My little hut in Tuaim Inbhir, a mansion would not be more delightful, with its stars as ordained, with its sun, with its moon.
>
> It was Gobán that has made it (that its tale may be told you); my darling, God of Heaven, was the thatcher who has thatched it.
>
> A house in which rain does not fall, a place in which spears are not feared, as open as if in a garden without a fence around it.

Ninth century Irish, trans.
Jackson, *Celtic Miscellany*, 72-3.

The place seems to mean 'Ivied tree-top'. Gobán was the legendary smith. It is ambiguous whether the 'hermitage' exists as a building or is a place open to the skies.

The poet Blathmac made the link between the natural world and the death of Christ

> *Ar-roichsiset mac nDé bí*
> *cethrae, alltai, ethaiti,*
> *ocus ro-coínset a guin*
> *cach míl fo-luigi lermuir.*

Tame beasts, wild beasts, birds had compassion on the son of the living God; and every beast that the ocean covers – they all keened him.

***Blathmac*, trans. Carney, stanza. 129, p. 45, on the death of Jesus**

To the right of the window-frame is a replica of the much later head with a bishop's, or abbot's, mitre, inserted into the wall from its original position. This replaces the one now in the outer wall of the Corofin Catholic church. It was carved by Risteard UaCroinín in about 1995, after the original head had been taken to Corofin Church. It seems likely that the original was a medieval representation of the sixth-century founder, Saint Blathmach, re-interpreted for its own century. Also on the south-east corner of the building is a carved corner stone, which has been reset into the wall on its side and so that only half of it is visible. In an oval frame a bearded figure is sitting on a stool, with his arms passing under his drawn-up legs and the hands clasped. Although reminiscent of the poses of some sheela-na-gigs, the purpose of this finely-carved and apparently clothed figure is a mystery.

The buildings we see today are from the Middle Ages. Like Dysert O'Dea, the site continued as a holy place after the church fell into ruin. We know little of the relations between the two sites in the past, where their lands lay or whether they were rivals in promoting their saints, but Rath is a peaceful place today with wide views across the Burren.

A demon badger, An Broc Sighe, is said to have been imprisoned in the lough by the Clare saint Mac Creiche (Mac Reithe), a friend of Blathmach. In 1318, banshees are said to have washed the clothes of the Normans about to be slain with their leader Richard de Clare. He had offended Saint Senan by pillaging Scattery Island, according to the fourteenth-century *Miracles of Senan*. The tower-house was one of those blown up by the Cromwellian forces in 1651.

Returning from this short road back to the junction, turn right and continue for three kilometres. Nearby on the

Fergus, though not on this route, was the site of the great battle of 1318.

This part of the way has various signs to other sites on a trail marked out by the Clare Archaeological Centre. This is based in the tower house at Dysert, some three kilometres on, where a café, toilets, exhibition and car-parking are to be found in summer.

Dysert O'Dea

This is also known by its older name, Díseart Tóla, the hermitage (desert) of Saint Tóla, whose death is recorded in AD 738. The name 'díseart' indicates that this was originally a hermitage, a desert in the forests of early Ireland, a place of solitary prayer. A small band of people dedicated to this lifestyle sometimes then gathered round to form a monastic settlement. This one is attributed to Saint Tóla, and has been a holy place for some 1,300 years. Perhaps eight hundred years ago, when the site was already old, the round tower was erected. The saint's feast-day was still remembered in the nineteenth century as 30 March but little else is recorded about him.

The current church ruins are from the twelfth century, about 500 years later than Saint Tóla, but still eight hundred years from our own time. A crozier from the same period is, like the one from nearby Rath, now in the National Museum. It is said that a bronze bell was found in the ground by the round tower and was used locally in about 1820.

The archway into the church with its sculpted heads is medieval. This spectacular group of carvings may be a reconstruction from more than one doorway, but the strange heads have been fitted harmoniously together. All the figures are unique, and many seem to have been

Carved heads at Dysert – Photo: Brendan Meegan

drawn from life, for the faces are full of character. Most are human, but there are several beasts, perhaps lions or oxen, with scrolls or batons in their mouths. Some of the human faces have beast-like characteristics, and one has a drooped nose like an eagle's beak. Another figure has a sweeping moustache. Whether some of the figures represent members of the monastic community at the time of carving, and whether there is an attempt to include the symbols of the Four Evangelists, it is impossible to say.

There are other carvings on the door, including two rams' heads, one of them damaged, and some delicate tracery. The doorway has a 'hanging eye' on the inside, for the wooden pole on which the door swung.

Inside the church, there is a beautiful east window with three lights, through which the high cross can be seen on a small hill. Much of the church was rebuilt and extended during its history.

Walking around the west end to the round tower, the outside of the west window can be seen, with its delicate carving.

The round tower is believed to be fairly late, and has ridges forming steps on the sides as it narrows. The enormous base, on a plinth at ground level, shows that it must have been very high when complete. The door is well above ground level. The tower was adapted over its life, and a later window was set into it near the top. It was fortified and also believed to have been ruined during the Cromwellian wars of the mid-seventeenth century. It was shored up in the nineteenth century, at a time when many landowners and antiquarians became interested in these buildings. The damage the tower has received shows the thickness of the walls.

There are family vaults in the churchyard, dating from the eighteenth and nineteenth centuries, when this form of family tomb was in fashion. A separate walled section of ground, outside the main churchyard and to the north, contains the well-preserved tomb of the Church of Ireland landowner Francis Hutchinson Synge, son of the evangelist Edward Synge whose bible with a bullet lodged in it is in Corofin Heritage Centre.

When Westropp visited in the 1890s he noted the roughly-carved cross with a circular head in the churchyard, but a font reported by earlier visitors had gone.

It is thought that medieval pilgrimages to Kilfenora started here and at Rath.

The High Cross

The High Cross is in the field to the east of the church ruins, accessible by a stile in the wall opposite the east gable. There are faint outlines in this field of what might have been the termon, the ditch and dyke boundaries of the monastic enclosure.

This cross was shattered by the Cromwellians, and re-erected in 1683 by Michael O'Dea as a sign on the base states in English. It was again repaired in 1871, under the auspices of the landowner Francis Synge. It is similar in style to the Kilfenora crosses.

At the apex is the figure of Christ, who is fully clothed, with his arms at right-angles to his body, in embrace or protection of the onlooker. Unlike the field cross at Kilfenora, Christ does not look over the monastery, but, at least as the cross has been re-erected, looks outwards. Below Christ is the larger figure of an abbot or bishop with mitre and crozier, also looking outward. This figure seems to be Saint Tóla, interpreted as a bishop in twelfth-century terms, with crozier and mitre in the design of that period.

Where his right arm should be is a carved hollow in the stone. This may have contained an arm which came outwards, either made of stone, or of bronze like the bronze arm-shrines known from elsewhere. If so, a relic of the saint may have been contained within it, so the arm-shrine might be taken out at times and used for blessing at a distance. If so, on one occasion it was not returned, or was stolen.

In later times, it is said that the head of the Christ figure was similarly taken around houses, in particular for relief against toothache. The current head is a replacement.

On one side of the cross are more carved figures, near the base. They may faintly be seen to be walking, perhaps in pilgrimage. There may be a tau cross at the centre of the group, which is perhaps being processed in honour of Saint Tóla.

The carving on the opposite side shows a break in style half-way up the shaft. It is possible that this is because the existing cross is actually formed from the broken pieces of two earlier ones, but carving with a similar break is known on crosses made of a single block of stone.

A holy well, dedicated to Tóla, is some distance away in the hollow of the field, near the wall. It was visited until the nineteenth century, and has recently been restored.

Behind the cross the gate leads to a path, and where this meets the road the left turn leads to the restored tower house with the visitors' centre.

To Ennis via Drumcliffe

Leaving from the Clare Archaeological Centre, and turning left through the gate leads after a kilometre to a T-Junction. Turning right for another kilometre on this road leads to another T-junction. The road entrance to Dysert site is now a kilometre to the right, but the turn left will bring the walker after another kilometre and a half to the main road, the R476.

The next 800 metres are on a busy and narrow road, especially for the first 100 metres. It then broadens around the quarry entrance for 500 metres, then narrows again. After another 200 metres, two minor roads meet at a junction on the left. Ignoring the first, signed for Ruan, and taking the second, unsigned, road for two kilometres leads to a T-junction. A turn left and then right over the bridge, around the tower house, leads to a road which continues straight for nearly three kilometres, to a T-junction. A turn right and a further two and a half kilometres' walk leads to Drumcliffe.

The ruined round tower can be seen for some distance before arrival. This early church site is only three kilometres from Ennis and near the flood-plain of the River Fergus. Little is known about it, but Drumcliffe shows something of how sites continued to be used, by the wealthy and by the anonymous poor.

The round tower has perhaps, like others, been subject to lightning strikes. More of it remained until two centuries ago, as a doorway and two windows were described in 1809. Beside it is a late medieval church with a window in the west gable taken from an older church from about 1200. At the top of the churchyard is the mass grave from a nineteenth-century outbreak of cholera, and close by in this area is a mass grave from the Great Famine of 1845-9. At the south-west end of the cemetery there is a large paupers' plot, where people from the Ennis workhouse were buried until relatively recently. A modern statue now commemorates them. A sign of the ways in which burials continue to be marked distinctively can be seen across the road in the modern cemetery, where there are some large and elaborate stones.

Taking the road with the site on the right and the modern cemetery on the left, there is a turn left after two kilometres onto the R352 and a further two and a half kilometres leads to the centre of Ennis, across the roundabout signed for 'town centre' and past the hostel. Ennis, 'island', originally Inis Cluain Ramh Fhada, 'island of the long rowing meadow', has a medieval Franciscan friary, and a museum containing items from across the county.

From Ennis south and west

The following route is suggested for those who wish to pursue a pilgrim trail. It links to Scattery Island, and many people in earlier times would have made the same link between places, where possible travelling by water. There are numerous minor church sites on or near it, and a sense can be gained of how the spirituality of people down the centuries has shaped the landscape. There are places that were of major importance in the past, like the abbey on Canon Island in the Fergus estuary; and there is also evidence of vernacular, local, religious practice, in the numerous holy wells, and in the cillíní, the 'little churchyards', which are the communal burial places of unbaptised and other young children. Some of these have been tended and signed in recent years.

This is also a way to see a lesser-known part of Clare, with the wide views over the Shannon estuary, which give a sense of how these sites were valued for their beauty over the centuries, and also how the river has been a hub of travel and trade. It is also a place from which much emigration has taken place, and a place where large-scale modern economic activity has also left its mark.

All these give something to reflect on through contemporary spirituality. It is suggested that the walker gives time to notice the sound and sights of the bird-life of both the land and the estuary; the treescape and the hedgerows; the changes along the coastline as the tide rises and falls; the taste of the salt on the wind; and the signs of animal and insect life.

By this route, it is some 70 kilometres from Ennis to Kilrush, from where a boat may be taken to Scattery Island. As a walking route it avoids busy roads as far as possible. However, the middle section follows the R373, which is for much of its length too narrow for safe or comfortable walking, so many might prefer transport for this part.

South of Ennis, Clarecastle is reached by the R473 which crosses the Ring Road, and gives a view of the ruins of the Augustinian Clareabbey. The community here had a Scattery Island connection, and may have been granted possession of the island in 1189.

Coming into the town, there is a Catholic church on the right, and immediately beyond it a stone memorial for those who died in the Great Famine of 1845-9.

Clarecastle is named after the castle that the Norman Richard de Clare built here in the years before his death in 1318 at Dysert O'Dea. Parts of it still stand beside the river. The Irish name is Clár eadar dá Choradh, the 'bridge between two weirs'. The castle stands at the head of the estuary of the River Fergus, which then joins the wider Shannon estuary. There are numerous islands, many of which have the remains of early Christian settlements, or are named in written sources.

The main road turns sharp left in the town but taking the right turn, the L4174 signed 'Mid Clare Way' takes the walker some eleven kilometres by minor roads through the low-lying pastures close to the Shannon.

After half a kilometre, the Mid Clare Way signs take the walker onto the L4172. There are several small roads leading off, but the route is marked by small yellow walkers' signs. The first part also contains signs for the Imeco Farm: at their entrance (which is a no-through road), the local road tales a sharp right and is signed. After another kilometre the route takes the right-hand turn, marked by the yellow Mid Clare Way sign. This is time turns sharp right again as it meets the river embankment.

From here, there are views of the islands in the Fergus estuary. Wading birds, including snipe can be seen, especially at low tide. Heron are also seen, especially at dawn or sunset. The embankments have been built up over centuries to protect the land and provide the pasture.

The Mid Clare Way route finally meets and crosses the R473. Not far overland, but not accessible from this route, are the ruins of Killone abbey, a medieval nunnery.

To continue to visit the pilgrim sites, it is worth leaving the Mid Clare Way and turning left onto the R473 to follow the right verge of the main road for 600 metres.

There is a right turn onto a minor road, marked for Kylea Graveyard. This is a further 600 metres, signposted on the left through the gate and farmyard for another 200 metres. There may have been an early church here, and the site gives a good view over the Fergus estuary and the nearby Horse Island. There is a holy well, which is not signed, in one of the fields.

Let us adore the Lord,
Maker of wondrous works,
Great bright heaven with
its angels,
The white-waved sea on
earth.

**Irish, possibly ninth
century. Trans. Murphy,
Early Irish Lyrics, 5.**

Back through the farm entrance and turning left back onto the road, a further 700 metres brings the walker to a left turn. This becomes part of the Mid Clare Way again, and passes around woodland and hedgerows, opening at times to a wider view as the road rises. After four kilometres there is a junction and the Mid Clare Way goes to the right. Taking the left, however, and following it downhill, continuing left at the next T-junction, leads to a narrow bridge. Crossing this and taking the sharp right turn leads after 200 metres to Clondegad Church.

This now-ruined Church of Ireland church was reputedly built on an earlier site. As is common with ancient sites, the churchyard contains both Protestant and Catholic burials. There is also a holy well nearby.

According to the *Ordnance Survey Letters* of 1839, the local tradition was that Saint Sgreavaun and Saint Feadaun lived in harmony in the church of Cluain-dá-Gad, the 'church of two withies'.

> The inhabitants of the parish have a traditional derivation for its name, and as I have no better authority on the subject I here give their version of the story: - St. Sgreavuan and St. Fiddaun both lived in the old church of Cluain-Da-Ghad (but by which of them it was built is not known) for a long time in peace and goodwill.
>
> They however, at length, quarrelled one day for the sole proprietorship of the establishment, and after a deal of angry feeling had been dissipated in some decent expressions of mutual reproach and contempt, they agreed to decide their dispute by a trial of sanctity and miracle-working power,

whereupon they cut a twig each and twisting them into gads, rolled them up into two rings which they cast into the river that runs down by the Church, first agreeing that he whose gad would go up against the stream should be declared the victor and owner of the Church.

No sooner than were the gads thrown into the stream than that of Fiddaun floated swiftly down with the current, while Sgreavaun's moved with greater velocity up against it, thereby proving him to be the more powerful and shewing Fiddaun that he was no match for him and that he should shift for himself somewhere else, whereupon he went some miles to the south-west and built a little Church for himself which still bears his name, Kilfiddan, while the name of Sgreavan has been sunk in perpetuating the medium of the miracle, and his residence is now called Cluain-Da-Ghad in place of Cluain Sgreavain.

Returning back to the junction at the bridge turn and continuing right down the larger road, after 800 metres from the church, the walker takes a sharp turn right onto a small road, just before the General Store. There is a crossroads after a kilometre, but continuing straight leads after another two kilometres to a T-junction. Here a cilín, a burial-place for children, is commemorated on the right. Turning left leads shortly to Kilchreest, the 'church of Christ', the remains of a medieval Augustinian foundation mentioned in 1189 as associated with Clare Abbey, and later with the monastery on Canon Island, until it was suppressed at the Reformation.

The view is over the islands of the Fergus estuary. As well as having so many small oratories and wells from the early Christian period, most of them were inhabited until fairly recently.

Nearest to the mainland is Deer Island, known historically as Inis Mór, the big island, on which Saint Senan is said to have founded a monastery. North of it is Coney Island, 'Rabbit Island'. This was previously known as Inisdadrum, Inis dá Droim, the island of two hills. It has the remains a small early Christian church on it. Some maps, however, give Inisdadrum as the little island off its southern end.

Inis dá Droim is the scene of an episode in the *Life* of Saint Brendan the Navigator, who is said to have founded a religious community here in about AD 550. This saint is also known as Brendan of Clonfert after the great religious site he founded there when in his eighties. The Latin account of his voyages in the Atlantic and the wonders he saw became a medieval bestseller and was translated into many European languages. Gerald of Wales in the 1180s called the Shannon estuary the 'Brendan Sea'.

Behind them is Canon Island, where a medieval foundation was built in the late twelfth century and became a major Augustinian abbey. Something of the economy of the area has emerged recently when changes in the course of the flow through the estuary uncovered the remains of large medieval fish-traps that were probably owned by the abbey. These were huge constructions of brushwood that jutted out into the estuary in a V-shape. The tide washed in fish and sometimes marine mammals, which were trapped in the funnel as the tide receded, to be harvested by the owners. There was evidence of similar practice from more ancient times.

There is a story that after the Reformation the monks of Canon Island hid from soldiers sent to make an end to the community. Finding the buildings empty, the soldiers departed. The monks emerged and rang their bells in joy, prematurely as it happened, for the sound carried across the water. The soldiers heard them and returned to destroy the monastery.

This road rejoins the R473 after another half kilometre at Ballynacally, and turning right here there is a shop, bar and accommodation. The name Baile na Cailli, means 'townland of the nun'. The word cailleach, in the genitive caillighe, here in its shortened form, means 'veiled one'. It is a loan-word from the Latin pallium, cloth or veil, but in modern Irish has come to mean 'old woman'.

The woodland here harbours a variety of small mammals, birds and many insects. The Irish, sessile, oak, which is suited to wet conditions, was common in early Irish woodlands, and place-names with the element 'derry' are often taken from the word dair, oak. Birds that make their homes here include tits, magpies, jays, goldcrests, warblers, chaffinches, blackcaps and tree-creepers. Among the mammals are red squirrel and pine marten, while fox, hedgehog and badger are common. There is rich plant-life below the trees. On the blanket bog inland, other plants and insects make their home. The Irish hare is common, and birds of prey may sometimes be seen above. Below, the Fergus estuary is important for over-wintering wildfowl, and for ducks and wading birds. The hedgerows have their own interests, and are full of the edible plants that were foraged until recently, including nettles, used for food, dyes and even fabric-making, blackberries, elderberry, sloes and other fruits. Various flowering plants include the large white bells of the bindweed, and the pink ones of the hedge bindweed. Fuchsia, a South American plant introduced for hedging in the eighteenth century, has become native. The delicate red hanging flowers are known in Irish as deoraí Dé, the 'tears of God'.

The next stage, on the R473, is on a road remarkable for its beauty but in many places too narrow to be ideal for walkers.

It is a further six kilometres to Kildysert, now a small town with shops and accommodation. On the way are views from the road over Canon and Coney Islands. In the village, the left turn signposted 'Library and Community College' leads beyond them and beside redundant buildings on the right to the church.

This dates from the Middle Ages when it was established as a parish church, though the name, which comprises 'cill', church, and 'díseart', hermitage, suggests an early Christian way of life here. The modern pier, a resting-place, is below the church. There is a Famine grave marked in the churchyard.

From Kildysert to Labasheeda, Leaba Shíoda, 'bed of silk', is thirteen kilometres along the coast on the R473. There are views over the Shannon estuary across to Foynes and the nearby Aughinish Aluminium Plant. Other signs of relatively recent activities that link this part of the world to the modern as well as the ancient include a stone set in an entrance five kilometres west of Kildysert. This reads: Sisters of St. Colomban – Founded Feb. 1922 – Went forth to China Sept. 1926. There is a stand of large, harvested oak trees on right.

The view over the estuary here includes Inishmurry. A recent book by Meaney and Elger describes life on the islands in the earlier twentieth century. As the road dips down to the estuary the smell of the coast and the mixture of the modern with the natural and with evidence of earlier lifestyles becomes evident.

In earlier times, the shoreline was foraged for shell-fish, which, especially in famine times, were a major source of food. Seaweed washed up or growing near the shore and harvested at low tide, was once an important source of food, fuel and fertiliser. In early Christian and medieval times, certain dyes for clothes, and even for manuscript illumination, were made from shellfish. Later, kelp was burnt for the production of iodine, which provided a much-needed cash-crop.

The sea has its own wildlife, and the Shannon estuary hosts a group of genetically-distinct dolphins, whose ancestors must have arrived many centuries ago.

Labasheeda is the 'bed of silk', a name taken from an earlier small local luxury industry. The road through the village leads to the peninsula, with an early church, holy wells and a Napoleonic battery at the point.

Passing straight on rather than turning, the main road has a right fork 900 metres from Labasheeda. This leads after two kilometres to Killofin Church, Cill Lua Finn, 'church of Lua the Fair', and its churchyard on the left. This is a late fifteenth-century church, with an eighteenth-century memorial within it. Surrounding it are many of the family burial vaults typical of West Clare.

Avoiding this detour, the route from Labasheeda continues on the R.473 signposted for Kilmurry McMahon (the 'MacMahon church of Mary'). The burial ground on the hill before the village is five kilometres further and has little to show of the foundations of a fifteenth-century church, nor of the nineteenth-century Church of Ireland church which was demolished in 1960.

After a further two kilometres, there is a left turn marked Knock, 'hill', and from here the route is easier for walkers again.

At Knock there is a resting place at the pier, where this view is over Clonderlaw Bay, and across the estuary to the economic aspects of contemporary life, as shown by Foynes and the aluminium works at Aughinish.

The road continues to Killimer, the church associated with a saintly sister of Senan. There is a ferry from here running across the Shannon, and bed and breakfast accommodation.

To continue the route without entering Killimer, about two kilometres after Knock on the Killimer road, and eleven kilometres from Labasheeda, there is a right-hand fork onto a minor road, which is marked 'Killimer GAA pitch'. Taking this brings the walker past a national school on the right and uphill for two kilometres and through a crossroads. At the next crossroads, some two kilometres further, taking the right turn, and after another 100 metres turning left, and then after another 900 metres left again (signed for Molougha church) brings the walker to the church.

Molougha church is early medieval, and is close to the reputed birthplace of Saint Senan.

The church site is dominated by the nineteenth-century vaults and grave-slabs. There is a holy well in the field to the east, approached through a stile from the churchyard, and now covered by a hawthorn tree. A recent stone from 1988 honours the fifteen-hundredth anniversary of Senan's birth, and has been erected on an older plinth.

The site overlooks Moneypoint power station below, and the village of Tarbert on the opposite side of the estuary. The huge powerstation is a startling reminder that electricity and greenhouse gases are generated here, from imported coal, and supply contemporary life here in the west. Tarbert means a 'place of bringing over' and is a

Psalm 16

Preserve me, God, I take refuge in you.
I say to the Lord: 'You are my God.
my happiness lies in you alone.'

He has put into my heart a marvellous love
for the faithful ones who dwell in his land.
Those who choose other gods increase their sorrows.
Never will I offer their offerings of blood.
Never will I take their name upon my lips.

O Lord, it is you who are my portion and cup;
it is you yourself who are my prize.
The lot marked out for me is my delight:
welcome indeed the heritage that falls to me!

I will bless the Lord who gives me counsel,
who even at night directs my heart.
I keep the Lord ever in my sight:
since he is at my right hand, I shall stand firm.

And so my heart rejoices, my soul is glad;
even my body shall rest in safety.
For you will not leave my soul among the dead,
nor let your beloved know decay.

You will show me the path of life,
the fullness of joy in your presence,
at your right hand happiness forever.

name often associated with ferry crossings. As with many places on the Shannon, there is a battery for guns intended to defend against the expected invasion by Napoleon's forces two centuries ago.

Continuing on the road past the church, a hundred metres further on is a signpost for Saint Senan's well and his reputed birthplace in a field to the left. Saint Senan's Lough is nearby.

Continuing on, there is a T-junction after a kilometre, and the right turn continues for another three and a half kilometres to a crossroads where it rejoins the R473. Turning left here it is a further two kilometres into Kilrush.

The name Cill Rois means 'church of the wood' or 'wooded height'. It was part of the termon, the protected holy space of the monastery on Scattery Island.

The ancient parish church here became a Church of Ireland church and is now a centre for traditional music. The Catholic Saint Senan's church has spectacular windows by the stained glass artist Harry Clarke (1889-1931).

Kilrush of course has accommodation, including a hostel, and also bars and restaurants, together with tourist attractions such as dolphin-watching and the Vandeleur Gardens.

Boats to Scattery Island leave from the Marina, at times which vary according to the tide.

A coast road leads beyond the Lifeboat Station to Cappa pier, two kilometres from Kilrush. There are views from here over Scattery Island with its round tower and the closer Hog Island. This road leads after six kilometres to the busy main road, the N67, past Moneypoint power station to Killimer and the ferry.

Alternatively, Loop Head to the west contains many ancient sites and places for reflection. Some are on the southern coast, parts of which are a cycle route. The lighthouse at Loop Head is open in, summer. The headland might once have been a sailing direction for Norsemen coming from Iceland, while the light will have been the last sight from Ireland for many emigrants.

The north coast has the rock formations of the Bridges of Rosses and wild cliff headlands, some of which were the sites of the promontory forts of the earliest inhabitants. Off-shore stacks and islands rise to sixty metres above the waves, and house many seabirds.

The most spectacular site is the inaccessible eighth-century ruin of the oratory on Bishop's Island, which rises sheer from the sea some five kilometres west of Kilkee. It gives a sense

Bishop's Island

of the adventure and the determination that led to the hermit life in early Ireland.

Cathedral on Scattery Island – Photo: R. Power

Section Three

SCATTERY ISLAND

SCATTERY Island, Inis Cathaigh, is three kilometres off Kilrush, in the Shannon estuary. It is the site of the sixth-century monastery said to have been founded by Saint Senan. It is remote in that it can become inaccessible from the mainland. It has always been, and remains, a place apart from, but in contact with, the wider world, on a key route for sea and river transport since ancient times.

There are many reminders of the past here, where the mainland traffic is also heard, where large boats sail the

Shannon, and planes can be heard arriving at and leaving the airport to the east.

In early Christian times and during the Middle Ages Scattery Island had a rich and complex monastic life like that of Kilfenora. There was the central round of prayer, and also the agricultural life, the work of craftspeople associated with the monastery, the visits of pilgrims to be accommodated. Study was part of the monastic round and perhaps manuscripts were made here, with all that processes this entailed.

Visiting today is very different. Kilfenora continued to have a church, which was adapted over the centuries, and a local community to surround it. On Scattery Island the buildings are more numerous but are in ruin, and the island is no longer inhabited, though it remains a place of pilgrimage. While almost nothing is known of Saint Fachtna, or of Inghean Bhaoith, there are many written sources, and some folk tradition about Senan, who remains deeply significant to the people of the area.

This suggested route around the island sites is not sufficient for a historical survey, but aims to offer some flavour of the complex history of faith on this island. Other resources include a website, which was set up with research by a Local Studies group, and contains some of the later folk tradition.

Traditionally, there were seven churches of Scattery, of which five remain, and there is also a ruined oratory. Most of the current ruins are medieval but they and older, vanished, buildings have been the focus of prayer and pilgrimage. Monastic life dates back to the sixth century. The round tower was built about four centuries later, at the time of the Vikings. A bell would have once sounded the call to prayer across the island. The largest church was first built before the Twelfth Century Reform, but has been added to many times.

There have been people living here until recently. It is a place where sounds of the mainland can be heard, but is a place too where over forty species of birds have been recorded, and there is unusual plant-life. There is a coastal lagoon, salt marsh, a freshwater lough and eroded sea cliffs on the western side. Rabbits, brought in by humans, also feed here, and some have become albino.

Saint Senan

Saint Senan is reputed to have been born nearby in Molougha in AD 488; to have founded several monasteries, the last of which was on Scattery Island; and to have died at a women's community on the mainland near Kilnagalliagh (Cill na gCailleach, 'Church of the Nuns') on 08 March, 544. This day has remained his 'patronal', feast day, and he is much celebrated in west Clare and along the Shannon.

He is credited with being one of the Twelve Apostles of Ireland, the male saints who took part in the christianisation of the island. As with other early saints, accounts of his life were written many centuries later, and are coloured by matters relevant to their own time. We therefore know very little about the saints themselves, but something about how they were regarded later. Senan is credited with being a local person who travelled widely, and was himself visited by other saints.

Senan's name seems to mean 'little old man', and therefore is similar to the many diminutive names found among the early saints, which seems to be marks of affection. Many ordinary Irish male personal names have a similar formation, and in modern Irish a baby was sometimes referred to jocularly as seanduine, 'old person'.

It has also been suggested that Senan's name is associated with the name Sionann, the Shannon, river itself, which is much celebrated in Irish mythology. Certainly, Saint Senan has been regarded as the patron and protector of the people of the estuary.

Senan's name appears with that of other saints in a number of written sources. Additionally, there are specific works associated with him, including a eulogy which may have been written in about AD 900. Senan's *Life* first seems to have been written in the eleventh century, and was the basis for both Latin and Irish versions which survive today. At this time the community of Scattery Island was hoping (unsuccessfully) to retain its status as the seat of a bishop. Senan continued to be highly regarded, and a collection of Miracles attributed to him was updated in the fourteenth century to include contemporary accounts.

Senan was the patron saint among the Corcu Baiscinn, the people who inhabited west Clare; and the Uí Fhidgeinte, who lived in around the Shannon estuary and inland into what is now County Tipperary. According to the accounts written long after Senan's death, Saint Patrick was asked to baptise among these peoples but declined, blessing the land and telling the people that there was a child in the womb who would preach to them instead.

His mother is sometimes said to have been the aunt of Saint Brigit of Kildare, while other texts name Senan as a son of Inghean Bhaoith of Killinaboy, and others as her nephew. His mother is sometimes credited with having forty-five children, among them several saints. Senan is reputed to have a saintly sister who gave her name to Killimer, and he is sometimes made a relative of a Bantry saint Cainnear (Cannera, Conaire).

There are a number of wells named after Senan along the Shannon and around Loop Head. One is at Kilkee some 12 kilometres away on the other side of the peninsular, and another near Carrigaholt was visited by boat from both the Clare and Kerry sides of the estuary. Other places associated with a Saint Senan, who may or may not be the Scattery Island saint, include the holy well close to the medieval church at Doonass, Kiltenanlea, near Clonlara in east Clare, on the Clare bank of the River Shannon north of Limerick.

Scattery Island is accessible by boat from Kilrush, at times the tides permit. In the past, pilots who guided ships up the river lived here. Some of the more recent pilots' families had moved to the island from Kilbaha in the nineteenth century. The role was an important one, as even the trip to Kilrush was difficult in poor weather, and the island was sometimes cut off for days. The pilot role meant that there was considerable knowledge of the wider world, gained from visiting seamen, and some Scattery men made a career at sea themselves.

The island may have been uninhabited when Senan came in the sixth century. The monastery was established and survived, though it was plundered in the Viking Age, and afterwards. There is nothing remaining from the original settlement, except some signs of the termon (from Latin terminus, boundary), the ditch and dyke enclosure round the central sacred space; and, perhaps the well close to the round tower.

The ruins of the cathedral and other churches are mainly from the twelfth and thirteenth centuries, and are now in State care, as is most of the island. The houses of the village are still standing but the final residents left in 1978.

Scattery Island – the name

The Irish name is Inis Cathaigh, the island of Cathach. Cathach is described in the Irish *Life* as a monster who occupied the island until driven out by Senan to whom it had been revealed that this was the place to build the monastery where he would be buried. The name is grammatically masculine and means 'battler'.

The name in English is a mystery. Earlier forms include Inisketty in a reference from 1189. A direct anglicisation of 'Cathaigh' might give Cathy, Caghy, or Cahy, but not Ketty.

A further difference between the English form and the Irish is the middle syllable 'er', which does not appear before the seventeenth century. Innuskatteragh alias Innuskattie was in use by 1660. Like the earlier versions, the name still retains the Irish words 'inis', island, which has been lost in modern centuries when the English 'island' was added after the name.

The last element in 'Scattery' might be the Norse 'ey', island. The first part of the modern name looks similar to the Norse word 'skatt(r)', meaning tribute or tax, but there is no satisfactory interpretation from a Norse point of view for the middle syllable.

One suggestion is that name is an oral interpretation meaning 'cantred of the Ostmen', that is the region ruled by the Norsemen. (*)

---

[*] Information summarised by Dr. Kay Muhr. See Breandán Ó Cíobháin, "Logainmneacha ó bharúntacht Mhaigh Fhearta, Condae an Chláir", *Dinnsheanchas* 1968-71 , esp. Pt 5, vol. vi (1970-1) 113-25, on Inis Cathaigh; and Dónall Mac Giolla Easpaig, "L'Influence Scandinave sur la Toponymie Irlandaise", in Ridel, Élisabeth, ed., 2002. *L'Héritage Maritime des Vikings en Europe de l'Ouest*, Caen, Presses Universitaires de Caen, 2002, pp. 441-482 .

It is not certain how the island got the English form of the name. It seems most likely that it comes from the Irish, and that the 's' of 'inis' has been taken over into the second word. The Norse 'ey' might have been added to the end.

The landing place

The pier is on the southern side of the island by the village. The stone seat beside the landing-place is inscribed with an account in English of how to perform the 'pattern', the 'rounds' of prayer once undertaken on the island by Catholic pilgrims.

One of the houses is now a small Visitors' Centre, open in summer. This guide follows a route anti-clockwise from the village, up the signed paths, then returning to the village and pier.

The sources for Saint Senan were written centuries after his death, so they are not historical sources so much as accounts of how Senan was regarded many centuries later, at times when his monastery remained a major religious site. They tell something about the concerns of their own times, and perhaps contain something of much older legends and the ways in which the island became holy.

The story of the founding of the island monastery, as told in the Irish *Life* and as translated in the literary style of the late nineteenth century, speaks of the vision and the Senan's arrival on the island while seated on a flagstone brought by an angel. There follows the expulsion of a monster and the blessing of the island, a blessing that saves people from being drowned at sea:

Then came Raphael the Archangel to commune with Senan, and he said: "Come with me, and I will shew thee the place in which thy resurrection will take place; for unto God it seems time for thee to reach it." Then Senan and the angel went till they were on Mullach Feis. Then said the angel to him: "Behold the island there. Thy resurrection shall be therein, and the resurrection of a great host of saints along with thee. In the west of the world there is. no more sacred island. No outrage to God hath ever been committed there. God sent an awful monster to keep it, so that neither sinners nor sons of cursing should dwell therein, but that it should remain in holiness awaiting thee. Yonder monster shall be put forth from the island before thee, so that dwelling along with it may not annoy thy community. For unto God it seemeth time for thee to go and build a church in that island. Noble and venerable will that church be. It will be a head of devotion and a well of wisdom of the west of the world. It will be a protection of prayer to foreigners and to Gael." Said Senan to the angel: "What seems timely to God seems timely to me; for this is what I seek continually, that which is the will of God."

With that the angels lift him up along with the flagstone on which he was sitting, from Mullach Fessi, and set him down on a high hill in the middle of the island; and thence is Ard na n-Aingel ('the Angels' Height'), and Lee na n-Aingel ('the Angels' Flagstone ') in Inis Cathaigh. They sing praise to God in that spot, even Senan and the angels, and then they went to seek the monster, to the place in which it abode.

When the monster heard them, it shook its head, and its hair stood up upon it, and its rough bristles; and it looked at them, hatingly and wrathfully. Not gentle, friendly, mild, was the look that it bestowed upon them, for it marvelled that anyone else should come to visit it in its island. So it went to them strongly and swiftly, insomuch that the earth trembled under its feet. Hideous, uncouth, ruthless, awful, was the beast that arose there. Longer was its body than Inis na h-Urclaide. A horse's mane had it an eye gleaming flaming in its head, and it keen, savage, froward, angry, edged, crimson, bloody, cruel, bounding. Any one would think that its eye would go through him when it looked upon him. Two very hideous, very thick feet under it; behind it a mane. Nails of iron on it which used to strike showers of fire out of the rocks of stone wherever it went across them. A fiery breath it had which burnt like embers. A belly it had like the bellows of a furnace. A whale's tail upon it behind. Iron, rending (?) claws upon it, which used to lay bare the surface of the ground on the path they came behind the monster.

Equally did it traverse sea and land when it so desired. Then the sea boiled from the greatness of its heat and from its virulence when it entered it. No boats could catch it: neither from that day to this has any one escaped from it who could tell tidings of it.

Now, when the monster came savagely to the place where Senan was biding, it opened its maw so that, as it drew nigh the cleric, its entrails were clearly seen over the maw. Thereat Senan lifted up his hand and made the sign of Christ's Cross in its face. Then the monster was silent, and this is what Senan spake to it:

"I say unto thee," saith he, "in the name of the Father, and of the Son, and of the Holy Ghost, leave this island and hurt no one in the district over which thou wilt go, nor in the district unto which thou wilt come." The monster went at once at Senan's word out of the island till it reached Dubloch of Sliab Collain. (*) And it did no hurt to any one, till it came there, nor after arriving; for it durst not oppose Senan's word.

Now after that Senan and the angels went righthandwise round the island till they came again to the Height of the Angels, after they had consecrated the island. Senan said to the angel: "Savage is the sea that there is around the island: there seemeth a troubled people therein." "Though it be savage," saith the angel, "whatever monk with

---

* That is, "black lough", near Inagh in County Clare.

humbleness of heart shall go from thee .... he will not be drowned until he shall come back to thee again." "God hath granted to thee," saith the angel, "that he over whom the mould of this island shall go, shall not be after Judgment an inhabitant of hell."

Then the angel uttered this stave:

> A sea high, stormy, past its side,
> not a royal element:
> No penance but death shall he taste,
> He over whom its mould goeth.

Senan seems to have needed a place free from tribal demands and the warrior culture. The *Life* goes on to show that defeating Cathach, the 'Battler', and protecting the monks from the sea is not enough. There follows a tussle, both physical and spiritual with the local king to retain his position there. The spiritual forces expressed in the monster were defeated but then came the human power games, which ended with the king's death.

The monster was longer than Inis na h-Urclaide, a name that suggests a long, narrow island with some form of dug ditch, perhaps one of the islands in the Fergus estuary which seem to have been closely connected with Senan's monastery on Scattery.

Whether the monster remained peaceful in its new home, the oldest account, the *Amra Senáin*, a praise poem from about AD 900, also refers to a monster, this time a female who lives in a lough. Taking a reference in the late eighth- or ninth-century poem *Féilire Oengusso*, which lists the saints and their feast-days, the poet says that the monster devoured a man who was under the protection of Senan, together with members of his household. The saint forced her to disgorge them unharmed, by hanging her, presumably by the fin, like a shark. There is a reminder to the audience of the biblical story of Jonah being swallowed and then belched out by a whale.

Saint Senan's bed

Walking counter-clockwise from the pier along the path, brings the visitor to the northernmost church, which lies a little apart from the main monastic site.

This isolated place, with views to the mainland and the modern wind-farms, contains a slab decorated with a cross; and a stone with an inscription in ogham, a native alphabet used for carving. There is a Romanesque church, with some decorative carving, perhaps from the later twelfth century.

Directly between the main church and the stones is a small plain oratory called St. Senan's Bed, where the saint is said to be buried.

The entrance has a metal bar across it, a reminder from the folk tradition that it is considered unlucky for unmarried women to enter. It is said that if they do they will never marry, or will never have children if they do marry. However, one oral account collected on the island in 1954 says that this does not apply to island women. There is also the story of an elderly woman who asked to be allowed to spend a night on Saint Senan's 'bed', where she was woken and blessed by the saint. (*)

Stones from St. Senan's Bed were taken as a protection against disease and especially drowning. It was a custom for seamen to carry a pebble from St. Senan's grave, and for island boats to carry them too.

---

* NFC 1358, collected from various informants, by Seán MacGráth, Kilrush in 1954, p. 389; NFC 1358, 351.

This site is outside the main monastic cluster, and it was perhaps a small secondary centre of activity in earlier times.

We know little of the life of the early monastic community, but it is likely to have been similar to that at Kilfenora, and other, coastal, communities. The island would have sustained the community, and perhaps also some ascetic monks who lived apart, elsewhere on the island. The day and night Offices would be said by the community, with particular emphasis on the *Book of Psalms*. This was often divided into three for daily recitation, and called the 'three fifties'. There were the Gospels and the rest of scripture to study and use in liturgy; and many additional prayers to be said. The *Miracles of Senan* says that there was a community of one hundred and fifty eating together each night, though this number may reflect the number of Psalms, and accordingly made it the ideal.

> Seven score psalm-singing elders
> In his household with great courses
> Without ploughing, without reaping, without drying,
> Without any activity except study.

There would also have been pilgrims and penitents, and the community would have been sustained by those engaged in manual labour. Clothing may have been basic, but over time the monks may have accrued lands beyond Scattery Island, which would have helped with provision for themselves and for visitors.

The island was then larger, as parts of the south and east have since been washed away. The soil is reasonably good for crops, and seaweed was available as fertiliser. There was also grazing and perhaps agriculture on the neighbouring Hog Island.

Pilgrimage by sea

Many of the stories of the early saints are entertaining, including those that suggest that if a pilgrimage is willed by God human needs will be provided for. But the stories also seem to contain warnings against going beyond one's physical and spiritual strength. This story in Irish was, like the Irish *Life of Saint Senan*, found in the late-medieval *Book of Lismore*. This survived because it was hidden away at some stage, and was found walled up in Lismore Castle, Waterford, in 1814.

> Three young clerics, of the men of Ireland, went on their pilgrimage. It was fervently and heartily they went. There was no provision taken to sea save three cakes.
>
> "I will bring the little cat," says one of them. Now when they reached the shoulders of the main, "In Christ's name," say they, "let us cast away our oars into the sea, and throw ourselves on the mercy of our Lord." This was done. Not long afterwards they came with Christ's help to a beautiful island. Plenty of firewood was therein, plenty of water. "Let us build a church in the midst of our island." This they do. The little cat goes from them. It draws to them a veritable salmon, up to three salmons for every (canonical) hour. "O God," say they, "our pilgrimage is no pilgrimage now! We have brought provision with us, our cat to feed us. It is sad now to eat his catching. We will not partake of the cat's produce." Thereafter they abode for six watches without food, until a message came from Christ that (some) was on the altar, to wit, half a cake of wheat for each man, and a piece of fish. "Well, then, let each of us make known his work for Him who feeds us."

The staple foods included a considerable amount of fish, including shellfish. Other foods found at monastic sites or mentioned in legal tracts include barley, black oats and the finer white oats. From these were made porridges, bread and barley beer. Wheaten bread was a relative rarity and used for special occasions and for sacramental purposes, as was imported wine. Green vegetables, brassicas, both of the salt-loving and the more cultivated types, such as cabbages, originally brought from Anglo-Saxon England, were part of the diet, and so were. edible seaweeds and herbs.

Bees were kept in places to provide honey for sweetening and for medicinal purposes. Both wild birds and their eggs were eaten, and hens were sometimes kept. Sheep were kept, and the wool used for clothing. On the island or nearby there would have been cattle, for milk, from which was made butter, a valued winter foodstuff. Calfskin was a basic material for vellum manuscripts. The slaughtering would have provided some meat, and the hides of older animals also provided leather. Inks for writing were made locally, but for more decorated manuscripts some of the coloured ingredients would have been imported. Other crops of the time included flax for linen and dyestuffs for clothing.

Much later, in the 1180's, the cleric Gerald of Wales, who came to Ireland with the Norman invaders, commented on the ways in which Ireland abounded in pasture but was poor in grain. It was also rich in fish and the Shannon in particular yielded the luxury food sea-lampreys. He also noted the belief that barnacle geese grew from shellfish and were eaten as fish during periods of fasting. Often a hostile commentator, he was respectful of the devotion of the Irish clergy to saying the liturgy. Many fasted all day and only ate when the 'work of God' was completed. However, he thought they then drank too much.

The legends concerning Saint Senan suggest a respect for, and wariness of, travel and its dangers. They also suggest contact with other monastic communities and their founders, and with the wider world.

In order to keep a sense of how the current buildings relate to many centuries of use, it is suggested that the visitor passes through the main monastic site with the round tower, and takes the grassed pathway just west of the main site, which is suited to barefoot walking, and that leads inland to Timpeall na nAingeal, the Hill of the Angels.

Hill of the Angels

A great earthquake is recorded in the annals for 16 March 804 and the monks gathered here as the earth shook.

The view from here covers most of the island, including the later Napoleonic battery and lighthouse, the eroding coast and other natural features. Below is the main monastic centre.

The church here is now very ruined, but it has the huge stones in the lower parts of the wall which suggest an early stone building. The story is that Senan first arrived on the island at this place, so it may have been from early times regarded as sacred, perhaps a place for reflection, some way from the main monastic site. Even in a strict religious community, like that founded by Senan, members sometimes went apart, to sanctified places, for reasons of penitence or to recover the sense of prayer.

High places are associated with angels, especially Saint Michael, as at Skellig Michael off Kerry, Mont Saint Michel in Brittany, and many others. This is the highest point of the island, but in the *Life of Saint Senan* it is not the warrior Archangel Michael who speaks with Senan here but Raphael.

In the *Life*, everything leads up to Senan's settling on Scattery Island. He was destined to preach in this part of the world by Saint Patrick. He travelled abroad, to Rome and to Saint Martin's monastery of Tours, and came home by way of Wales, where he visited Saint David. After his return, he established several monasteries; is associated with two nunneries; and finally founded his chief monastery here on Scattery Island. He remained in contact with other early saints, and, although the monks lived an austere life, he lived to a fine age, dying in his mid-fifties.

Senan's personal reputation is rather mixed. The numbers of holy wells associated with his name suggest he was popular down the centuries among local people. He was not only powerful and local, but was considered kindly.

The written sources, however, suggest that it was unwise to cross him, as this was equated with crossing God's will. Some of this may relate to the politics of the time of the writers, who were seeking to ensure that the status of Scattery Island was upheld at times of change. The *Life*, written in the twelfth century, though it refers to the sixth century, speaks of the king who opposed him and met his end.

Others who violated his sanctuary suffered for it. *The Miracles of Senan*, a collection expanded in the early fourteenth century, when the island was again seeking to be the centre of a diocese, names powerful people of that time like Richard de Clare, who suffered after wronging Senan. The saint remained a powerful protector.

By the time the accounts were written, the Vikings had been and gone, much violence had occurred, and there were probably laypeople on the island as well as the monastic settlement. Perhaps some of the stories relate to these changes. For all the love shown for Senan, another aspect of his character, his relations with women, is at first sight not attractive.

He is, for example, presented as hard on his mother. When only a small child he rebuked her for eating blackberries between meals.

As well as being associated with the nuns at Kilnagalliagh, according to the Irish *Life* he was asked by the daughters of the king of the Uí Fhidgeinte, who had taken to the religious life, to be their bishop. As nuns in early Ireland were subject to bishops, Senan's duties to them may have been in conflict with his desire for an austere male monastic life. His relations with holy women may be influenced by memories down the centuries of the tensions such a situation could arouse.

The kindlier side is evident in the tale of Saint Brigit of Fennish Island near Kilconry (the church of Connaire) in the Fergus estuary, who sent him a gift in a basket she made. It came ashore at Scattery Island, and Senan sent a gift back by the tide in the same basket. The gifts are liturgical or sacramental, and perhaps indicate something of the sharing that is the ideal. The story may have served to impress on the reader the status Senan held, but it also draws attention to the story of Moses hidden by his mother in a basket of rushes and found there by Pharaoh's daughter. The story is preceded in the Irish *Life* by an account of two of the Twelve Apostles of Ireland, Brendan and Ciarán coming to seek spiritual advice from Senan as a soul-friend. As a bishop he was regarded as their senior in the spiritual life.

Inghean Bhaoith, the saint of Killinaboy, that some sources names his mother or aunt, engages with him very much as an equal in an eleventh-century poem. Before the end there will be women on your island she declares. (*) Perhaps, between pilgrims and residents there were by the time the poem was written.

Another saint, Cainnear (*Canair,* now often spelt Connaire, also Cannera), who is sometimes seen as a relative, was more forthright. In the medieval Latin metrical (verse) *Life of Senan,* his resolution not to admit any women is even extended to this saint, although Cainnear had been brought to the island by an angel. Senan declares that women had nothing to say to monks and neither she nor any other would be allowed on the island.

Rebuttals of this kind no doubt annoyed people in the past, and the vigorous response of Cainnear herself as told in the Irish *Life of Saint Senan* may be a rebuff to an overwhelming use of clerical power.

---

* Grosjean and O'Keefe, *Irish Texts* iv, poem v, verse 9.

Cainnear (*Canair*) was a nun of Bantry called *chráibhtheach*, the 'holy', who had a vision of all the churches of Ireland sending prayer up to heaven like towers of fire. The greatest fiery tower was that of Scattery Island. She felt that here was the place of her death and burial, the 'place of her resurrection'.

Straightway on she went, without guidance save the tower of fire which she beheld ablaze without ceasing day and night before her, till she came thither. Now, when she had reached the shore of Luimnech [Limerick], she crossed the sea with dry feet as if she were on smooth land, till she came to Inis Cathaig [Scattery Island]. Now Senan knew that thing, and he went to the harbour to meet her, and he gave her welcome.

"Yea, I have come", saith Canair.

"Go", saith Senan, "to thy sister who dwells in yon island in the east, that thou mayest have guesting therein."

"Not for that have we come", saith Canair, "but that I may have guesting with thee in this island."

"Women enter not this island", saith Senan.

"How canst thou say that?" saith Canair. "Christ is no worse than thou. Christ came to redeem women no less than to redeem men. No less did He suffer for the sake of women than for the sake of men. Women have given service and tendance unto Christ and His Apostles. No less than men do women enter the heavenly kingdom. Why, then, shouldst thou not take women to thee in thine island ?"

"Thou art stubborn", saith Senan.

"What then, saith Canair", shall I get what I ask for, a place for my side in this isle and the Sacrament from thee to me?"

"A place of resurrection", saith Senan, "will be given thee here on the brink of the wave, but I fear that the sea will carry off thy remains."

"God will grant me", saith Canair, "that the spot wherein I shall lie will not be the first that the sea will bear away."

"Thou hast leave then", saith Senan, "to come on shore." For thus had she been while they were in converse, standing up on the wave, with her staff under her bosom, as if she were on land. Then Canair came on shore, and the Sacrament was administered to her, and she straightway went to heaven.

God granted unto Canair that whoso visits her church before going on the sea shall not be drowned between going and returning.

The story, unmatched in medieval Irish literature, gives an insight on several levels. The round towers reach to heaven as a symbol of prayer rising like the flames of an Old Testament sacrifice. They also provide a beacon for the travelling saint like the pillar of fire that led Moses and the Israelites through the desert.

The role of Senan as a bishop is significant, for he is seen, albeit reluctantly, as doing his duty towards a nun.

The core is the statement of the equal value of women to men in God's eyes, including their equality in a life of prayer and service. Like an earlier male saint in the *Life,* Cainnear's place of burial and resurrection on the last day will be preserved by God, even on this eroding island.

There may even be a reference to the story of the Gentile Syro-Phoenician woman in the Gospels, who persuaded Jesus to heal her daughter (Matthew 15:21-8, Mark 7:24-30). Senan is emulating Christ by allowing a woman to successfully argue her case. The fact that the passage is included in a *Life* not of Cainnear but of Senan, suggests

112

I pray you, Christ, to change my heart
To make it whole;
Once you took on flesh like mine,
Now take my soul.

Ignominy and pain you knew,
The lash, the scourge,
You, the perfect molten metal
Of my darkened forge.

You make the bright sun bless my head,
Put ice beneath my feet,
Send salmon leaping in the tides,
Give crops of wheat.

When Eve's wild children come to you
With prayerful words,
You crowd the rivers with fine fish,
The sky with birds.

You make the small flowers thrive
In the wholesome air,
You spread sweetness through the world
What miracle can compare?

Irish, eighth century, trans. Kennelly, printed Murray.

that the biographer thought that it reflected on Senan's sanctity, even though on this occasion he met his match.

Oral versions derived mainly from the printed version and influenced by a ballad of Thomas Moore's (which sits very lightly to the legend) were collected in the 1950s, not long before the island was abandoned. These are derived from the written source, but Senan is less courtly in his riposte, and Cainnear's walking on the water is omitted. She rather than Senan arrives by flagstone. Trying to land on the island:

'I'm going to die, I'm going to die', she shouted at him, but all to no avail. Senan shook his fist at her and was about to walk away when she said to him: 'When our Lord died on the cross', she says, 'he died for women as well as men'. But even this didn't soften him.

She is allowed the Eucharist, however, is buried at the furthest spot on the foreshore, which is uncovered only once a year when the spring tide is at its outset ebb.

Stones from her grave as well as Senan's have power to prevent drowning. (*)

The name 'The Lady's Grave' is still used for a flagstone seen at low tide on the eastern shoreline beyond the Napoleonic battery.

The monastic centre

The next stage is the tower, and the ruins on the central site of the monastic enclosure. The heart of the monastery was sacred space, and originally small timber buildings, chapels, living quarters, perhaps a scriptorium

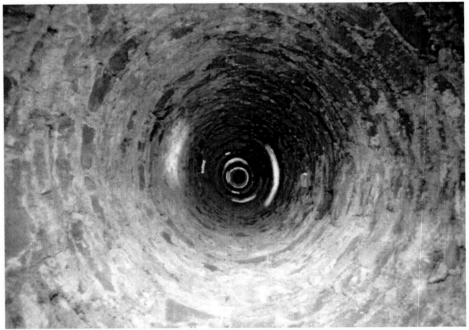

Interior of the round tower – Photo: B. Meegan

for writing, and a shrine to hold relics would have stood here in this central space. None of these buildings remain and only a few faint marks in the grass show the curve of

---

* Austin MacMahon, NFC 1358 (1954), 349,

Be thou my vision, O Lord of my heart,
Naught is all else to me, save that Thou art.

Thou my best thought by day and by night,
Waking or sleeping, Thy presence my light.

Be Thou my wisdom, Thou my true word;
I ever with Thee, Thou with me, Lord.

Thou my great father, I Thy dear son;
Thou in me dwelling, I with Thee one.

Be Thou my battle-shield, sword for the fight,
Be Thou my dignity, Thou my delight.

Riches I heed not, nor man's empty praise,
Thou mine inheritance now and always.

Thou, and Thou only, first in my heart,
High King of heaven, my treasure Thou art.

King of the seven heavens, grant me for dole,
Thy love in my heart, Thy light in my soul.

Thy light from my soul, Thy love from my heart,
King of the seven heavens, may they never
depart.

With the high king of heaven, after victory
won,
May I reach heaven's joys, O bright heaven's
sun!

Heart of my own heart, whatever befall,
Still be my vision, O Ruler of all.

**Ninth century. Trans Mary Byrne, versified
Eleanor Hull.**

the protective enclosure. Nearby would have been other buildings, for hospitality, and for the craft workers that were attached to the larger monasteries. Some of the buildings may be based on older foundations, but the oldest standing may be the tower. Raised in the ninth or tenth century, it has stood over a thousand years against the wind, in Cainnear's vision, the highest tower of prayer in Ireland. It is visible from far out to sea, and the bell rung from the top, where there are four windows under the conical roof, is said to have been audible on both sides of the Shannon. Its role was to bless to the land over which it was heard and to enable the hours of prayer to be kept by all at the same time. A bell, Clog an Óir, the bell of gold, which may be a bronze bell now in the British Museum, together with its shrine, now in the National Museum of Ireland, was a noted relic of Saint Senan, perhaps made in his honour at some time in the island's history.

> The sweet little bell that is rung on a windy night, I would rather go to it than to meet a wanton woman. (Jackson, *Celtic Miscellany*, 136)

Gerald of Wales in the late twelfth century remarked on how bells, and the staffs of saints, were revered. There are other windows in the tapering tower. It is one of only two in Ireland where the entrance is at ground level, flush with the foundations of the tower. It is also believed to be one of the earliest and is one of the tallest, and is almost complete.

The bases of the wooden floors that would have once stood within it can be seen. When in use these floors may have been filled with items needing a safe place of storage, relics, items left by patrons, foodstuffs to be kept dry and away from mice.

This tower has acted as way-marker for pilgrims and for seafarers across the Shannon, and for those coming from the Atlantic into Limerick. It was the last sight for thousands who, during the Cromwellian period, were sent to work in the plantations of the Caribbean; of those who left during the Famine years; and of those who left by sea in the years of emigration since.

One oral account from later times gives to us what is a quite different attribution. Under the round tower is an entrance to Cathair na gCat, the city of cats, where bad priests go and become cats after death. They hear the liturgy chanted by the ancient monks, but cannot join in. The chanting of the monks it was said could also be heard at the Daimlaig, Senan's grave, between sunrise to sunset. (*)

St. Senan's Well

The well lies about 20 metres west of the Round Tower. This is the place where, the *Life* tells us, an angel told Senan during a drought that he would find a source that will never run dry and will serve to heal all illnesses. Senan dug, using a holly branch, which he then planted. By the next morning, there was a well full of water and a holly tree stood beside it.

It is also possible that the water-source predates the monastic settlement, and that perhaps this is why this particular site was chosen.

Twentieth-century oral tradition collected on the island noted that the well never ran dry and that foreign sailors used to come ashore to take water to carry with them to allay storms at sea.

The cathedral

This fine church, large by Irish standards, was built for the benefit of secular visitors as well as a monastic community. It seems to have been started before the church reforms of the twelfth century and to have been rebuilt and extended several times. At one time it would have been full of decoration and can be imagined roofed, with wall-paintings and other aids to the imagination.

---

* NFC 1356 (1954), various tellers, 389-90.

> **Psalm 126**
>
> When the Lord released Sion from bondage
> it seemed like a dream.
> Then was our mouth filled with laughter,
> on our lips there were songs.
>
> The heathens themselves said: "What marvels
> the Lord worked for them."
> What marvels the Lord worked for us!
> Indeed we were glad.
>
> Deliver us, O lord, from our bondage
> as streams in dry land.
> Those who are sowing in tears
> will sing when they reap.
>
> They go out, they go out, full of tears,
> carrying seed for the sowing:
> they come back, they come back, full of song,
> carrying their sheaves.

Scattery Island had bishops that trace themselves as heirs of Saint Senan. During the Viking Age, the island served as the church centre of an area that encompassed the Norse town of Limerick. However, the diocese set up after the Synod of 1111, under the auspices of the powerful king Muirchertach Ua Briain, had Killaloe at its centre, in his ancestral heartland. This church on Scattery Island is known as the cathedral, though it was never the mother-church of a separate diocese.

Like many such Irish churches, it stands near the round tower, though not as close as most, which have the tower just to the north-west. It has early features for such a large building, including the projecting antae of stone at the west gable. As at Killinaboy, these are reminiscent of the earlier timber buildings with overhanging ends. It also has a west, trabeate, doorway, as well as the later arched door on the south wall.

This large church was the main place of worship in later times. It contains fine carved stones that show something of the grandeur it must once have had. There is also a small vestry or chapel on the north side.

The ruined but beautiful east window catches the rising sun and points across Ireland and beyond to Jerusalem, the place of the Resurrection of Jesus. Once the main altar stood below it.

Perhaps one of the most startling aspects when visiting today is that this window now frames Moneypoint Power Station. This can raise complex aesthetic responses, together with views on issues of justice in an interconnected world, the nature of generated power, the arrival of coal to fire it from across the world and the conditions in which it is mined and shipped. It is particularly poignant here in Scattery Island where wind farms on the mainland can also be seen.

On the outside of this window are medieval carvings, including two animal heads, and in the centre the head of a mitred bishop, carved in the later middle ages, and another example of the ways in which Senan was interpreted for later centuries.

The building may rest on older foundations, as does the small oratory immediately to the north of the cathedral. This shows Romanesque features dating from the twelfth century and it may have been built over an older chapel that held relics. This site, now peaceful and cared for, has been visited by many people over the centuries, not all of them benevolent. There has been much violence here, perpetrated by people both foreign and Irish. A ninth-century Irish poet wrote:

> Bitter and cold the wind tonight
> It tosses the waves' white hair
> Tonight I fear not the fierce Vikings
> Coursing the wild sea.

119

The Vikings from Scandinavia were plunderers and slavers, and later also traders and settlers, who established towns like Limerick and gradually blended into Irish society.

The 'heathens' were in Ireland by AD 795 when Iona in the Hebrides, Inishmurray and Inisbofin were plundered without warning. The *Annals of Inisfallen* say that they were back the following year. Scattery Island may have escaped the earliest raids and had time to make some plans for defence, or escape, but the monastery was raided and destroyed by Vikings in 816, when many people were killed, and again in 835.

The Irish Annals record many other attacks in these years, such as those on the great monastery of Bangor in the north, in 823 and 824. Poignantly, the isolated hermitage of Skellig Michael off the coast of Kerry was also attacked in 824, and one Étgal was carried off into captivity, and he died of hunger. Inland Ireland also suffered, with the Norsemen making use of the River Shannon and establishing themselves at Limerick. Yet we also hear of abbots and bishops of Scattery dying peacefully throughout the Viking years.

After a hundred years there may have been respite for a generation or so. Then, in 922, Tomair son of Elgi, one of the leaders of the Limerick Norse settlement, plundered along the Shannon, burnt Clonmacnois and raided in Meath. Forty-five years later, in 967, Limerick and its ships were burnt in turn.

If the monks were not expecting attack when they raised this tower during these years, it was perhaps because they were colluding with the Norse traders of Limerick, and perhaps also with bands of raiding Vikings.

With the rise of the Munster Dal Cáis dynasty comes evidence of attempts to control the Limerick Norse and indeed in 972 to banish them. In 974, Ívarr, leader of the Limerick Norse, fled to Scattery Island, which suggests it has an established connection with Limerick. If he expected to be safe there he was mistaken, for Magnús, son of Aralt (in Norse Haraldr), plundered the island and captured Ívarr, violating the sanctuary rights of the island, and the protection accorded to the foundation of Saint Senan. Ívarr escaped overseas the next year, but also in 975 the Dal Cáis king Brian, later of Clontarf fame, plundered Scattery Island. He also successfully attacked Limerick that year. Two years later, Brian killed Ívarr and his two sons in the sanctuary of Scattery Island. Thirteen years later, in AD 990, Brian ransomed another prisoner on Scattery Island. We also hear during these years of two more natural deaths of senior clerics on the island. Monastic life went on, whatever compromises has been made.

These events were not easily forgotten. The poem in which Inghean Bhaoith tells Senan that there will be women on his island is one of a surviving handful which indicate how seriously the violation of sanctuary was taken. According to the *Annals of Loch Cé*, on the night before the Battle of Clontarf in 1014, two men, retainers respectively of Brian and of the king of the Corcu Baiscinn, who was also involved in the 977 violence, had visions. In these, a group of clerics led by Saint Senan appeared to them and demanded compensation for the attack on Scattery Island. Brian's retainer protested that Senan would have got it had he stayed at home, but the response was that the payment would be required the next day. Both kings were slain at Clontarf. Even *Cogadh Gaedhel Re Gaillaibh*, the 'War of the Irish with the Foreigners', a laudatory account of Brian's activities, written a hundred years after the Battle, also recognises that its hero Brian broke the sanctuary of the island.

So Scattery Island was a place of continuing monastic life, but also a political pawn in the power-games of the time, especially those concerning Limerick. It was a place for hostages to be held, and it seems impossible that the monastery was not involved with the trade in captives. The island may have had a substantial population, some of it transitory. The community or its associated lay members may have acted as pilots. As the Norsemen adapted to the ways of the Irish, its position as a church centre was again recognized, a place where secular and spiritual power came together. The booty that passed this way may have included many unfortunate people on their way to slavery elsewhere, as well as works of craft and writing.

The poetry in which Senan extracts payment, and is yet challenged himself, may have undertones of monastic collusion between Norse and native powers. Something similar may lie behind Inghean Bhaoith's taunt that before the end there would be women on the island, for some may have come not as pilgrims but as captives. The ideal of the settlement dedicated solely to God had been sullied by its commercial use by Vikings, and the monastery's dealing with them had led to unforeseen consequences.

The light of my heart is your heart, O Saviour,
the treasure of my heart is your heart poured out for me;
since it is clear that your heart is filled with my love, O beloved,
in my innermost heart leave your heart for safe-keeping.

What you have suffered on our account, O mighty and splendid High King,
my thoughts cannot determine nor account for;
it is the hot piercing hurts in your heart and your sores, O beloved,
which urge the wise in their thousands to their reward. ...

When I return again by your leave, O flower of the Orders,
to Christ's sanctuary and with the covering of his grace to protect me,
the rough stony heather-hills that troubled me before
will become smooth silken plains and fields of satin.

Even though you were astray, O fair holy King from heaven,
tormented in our midst in a way that cannot be estimated,
you made no boast of your love for us, O Christ, till the lance tore open
a haven in your heart for the whole world.

Tadhg Gaelach Ó Súilleabháin (c.1715-95), trans. Kinsella, in Mac Murchaidh, Lón Anama, 246-7.

The violence did not end with the Viking Age, though it became more sporadic. The *Annals of Inisfallen* state the island was attacked in 1057 by 'foreigners', Norsemen, who plundered and slaughtered. They were allied to Irish kings, and this is part of an Irish picture. Scandinavians may be held responsible when in 1101, pirates came from the north, 'and they destroyed Inis Cathaig, taking many valuables from it, and committed many other evil deeds.' They were probably followers of Magnús Barelegs, king of Norway, who intended conquest in Ireland.

Later that century, the Anglo-Norman invasion of Ireland led to new dynamics.

The English were driven out of Limerick by the Irish Ua Briain, but then later the rulers of Limerick reasserted their authority over Scattery in 1176. Three years later in 1179 the Anglo-

Norman William Howell laid the island waste. Richard de Clare plundered before his death at Dysert O'Dea in 1318. He seems to have regarded the island as his by conquest, for it is among the lands claimed by his sister, who was his heir.

The Church of the Dead

Returning towards the village street, on the right is Timpeall na Marbh, the Church of the Dead. This later church, perhaps originally built in the thirteenth century, was used as the islanders' burial place. Part of the cemetery may have been taken by the sea as it continues to erode the island. There are many gravestones from the eighteenth and nineteenth centuries. Some of these have carved on them the symbols of Christ's Passion, a hammer and pliers, a cock, thirty pieces of silver, and the sun and moon.

In the village street is a reminder of the other inhabitants of the island and gives a sense of how a small Irish community looked in the earlier twentieth century. The landing place for the island has remained much the same down the years.

The ruined tower house, the Castle, is sixteenth century, but built on older foundations. There is said to have been an earlier castle built by Brian Borúma. This fortress was built by an Ó Carthaigh ruler to defend access to Limerick and the River Shannon. It may have used using stones from churches that were already in ruin.

There is a path at the far end of the village to the lighthouse and Napoleonic battery. The walk gives a chance to appreciate some of the island's wildlife, the birds, plants, salt marshes and coastline. However, the path can be cut off by high tides due to an artificial inlet.

The threat of a possible French invasion of Ireland and then of Britain at the beginning of the nineteenth century was taken seriously. The remains from this time of fear can be seen here on Scattery Island and along both sides of the estuary, in the huge batteries, defences built against an enemy who never came. The lighthouse, automated some years ago, was built in the nineteenth century, to protect and guide shipping.

In former times a strenuous pattern was undertaken on Scattery Island, both by islanders and visitors. It was suppressed by Catholic authorities in the mid-nineteenth century because there was drunkenness as well as prayer at such events, but the pattern continued in the hands of the people.

Walking the 'rounds', on Scattery Island, was a particularly hard devotional experience. According to an account recorded in 1954, the whole pilgrimage involved walking barefoot along the shoreline of the entire island five times on the fifth day of the week, Thursday. There were various stopping places, which were circled while saying special prayers. At the end of the first four rounds of the island, the pilgrim prayed at one of the surviving churches, and after the fifth round prayed while circling the round tower. The pilgrim then drank from Saint Senan's well. The pattern was not particularly observed on Senan's feast day in March, but some people tried to do the pattern on five successive Thursdays, and everyone who lived on the island tried in their lifetime to do the rounds at least once.

Scattery Island remains a place of spirituality on the margins, an island on the edge of Ireland, where prayer and piloting both occurred down the centuries. The stories of people who survive and the stories that survive against the grain are part of the spiritual heritage that, together with respect for the natural world, are the legacy for future generations.

Perhaps the story of Saint Cainnear's grave still surviving the encroaching waves speaks to people on the margins whose situations may be obliterated by the waves of indifference, but those whose story is central to the Christian understanding of humanity.

Conclusion

ACCORDING to a short poem, often associated with a female saint, Brigid, Íde, or Samhthann,

> Going to Rome
> Great the trouble, little the gain
> When the king you desire
> Is not brought on the road with you.

The *Life of Samhthann*, abbess of Clonbroney, says that she told people that pilgrimage is of no use unless we carry the purpose, God, with us: we can reach the kingdom of heaven from any land. Inghean Bhaoith, the saint who came to connect the sites from Kilfenora to Scattery, is attributed with foretelling a future open to the unexpected.

This book has aimed to provide some taste of the pleasures of walking around and between ancient sites, to appreciate the land and value the history of these stopping places and their significance to people of the past. They have given much pleasure to those who visit and sense something of what they have meant over the centuries.

In terms of what we see and how we interpret the sites, we have the physical remains. They carry the marks of changes over many centuries of re-use and reinterpretation, of how best to create the space for prayer, and sanctuary, at the centre of Christian

127

community. In the case of some saints, like Senan, we have also the writings, accounts of their lives and actions adapted over centuries to fit the mood and perceived needs of their times. We also have the anonymous poetry that expresses the exploration of the spiritual in different ways and in different times.

There is no single interpretation of any place, or of the impact of any one saint, because we are heirs to the accretions of centuries during which change and prayer have taken place. We are part of that process as we rest in these places and listen to the stories today, told and heard in ways influenced by our own times and concerns.

A pilgrim walk is a personal experience, one that develops as it is undertaken, and which engages with people met on the way. Above all, it has the capacity to be a journey of self-discovery, and it can transcend this, and become a spiritual experience.

There are places to stop and reflect, but the act of walking and stopping, alone or in company, is central. It provides a chance to take time to observe and enjoy creation, in all its manifestations and in all the weather that can change any outlook, that can give us new insights into the power of nature and its beauty, into the past and into ourselves. The knowledge that many people have done this before us is part of the gift.

In walking we seek to leave no trace but in our memories, and in the delight we experience, alone or together, which in some indefinable sense carries a blessing to those who walk and rest after us.

'Written by Colman the Irishman to Colman returning to his own land'

So, since your heart is set on those sweet fields
And you must leave me here,
Swift be your going, heed not any prayers
Although the voice be dear.

Vanquished art thou by love of thine own land,
And who shall hinder love?
Why should I blame thee for thy weariness,
And try thy heart to move?

Since, if but Christ would give me back the past,
And that first strength of days,
And this white head of mine were dark again,
I too might go your ways.

Do but indulge an idle, fond old man
Whose years deny his heart.
The years take all away, the blood runs slow,
No leaping pulses start.

All those far seas and shores that must be crossed,
They terrify me: yet
Go thou, my son, swift be thy cleaving prow,
And do not quite forget.

Hear me, my son; little have I to say.
Let the world's pomp go by.
Swift is it as a wind, an idle dream,
Smoke in an empty sky.

Go to the land whose love gives thee no rest,
And may Almighty God
Hope of our life, lord of the sounding sea,
Of winds and waters lord

Give thee safe passage on the wrinkled sea,
Himself thy pilot stand,
Bring thee through mist and foam to thy desire
Again to Irish land.

Live, and be famed and happy: All the praise
Of honoured life to thee.
Yea, all this world can give thee of delight,
And then eternity.

Ninth century Irish poem in Latin, probably composed in a continental monastery. Translated Waddell, Medieval Latin Lyrics, 84-5, 314-5.

Bibliography

1. Sources for poetry translations

Carey, John. King of Mysteries: Early Irish Religious Writings. Dublin, Four Courts, 2000.

Carney, James, ed. and trans. The Poems of Blathmac son of Cú Brettan. Dublin, Irish Texts Society, 1964.

Clancy, Thomas Owen and Gilbert Markús. Iona; the Earliest Poetry of a Celtic Monastery. Edinburgh, University Press, 1995.

Jackson, Kenneth. A Celtic Miscellany, Harmondsworth, Penguin, 1971.

Meyer, Kuno. Selections from Ancient Irish Poetry. London, Constable, 1911.

Murphy, Gerard. Early Irish Lyrics, eighth to twelfth century. Oxford, Clarendon Press, 1956.

Murray, Patrick, ed. The Deer's Cry: a Treasury of Irish religious verse. Dublin, Four Courts Press, 1986.

MacMurchaidh, Ciarán. Lón Anama: Poems for Prayer from the Irish tradition. Dublin, Bord na Leabhar Gaeilge, 2005.

O'Connor, Frank. A Book of Ireland. Glasgow, Fontana/Collins, 1959.

Psalms. The Psalms: The Grail translation. London, Harper Collins, 1963, revised 1995.

Waddell, Helen. Medieval Latin Lyrics. Penguin Classics, Harmondsworth, 1929.

2. Other works

Annals of Loch Cé. Ed. William Hennessey, Rolls Series 54, 1871. www.ucc.ie/celt

Annals of Inisfallen, ed. Seán Mac Airt. Dublin, 1951. www.ucc.ie/celt

Annals of the Four Masters. Ed. John O'Donovan, 5 vols., 1848-51. www.ucc.ie/celt

Annals of Ulster (To AD 1131), ed Seán Mac Airt and Gearóid Mac Niocaill, Dublin 1983. See also translation on www.ucc.ie/celt

Arensberg, Conrad M. and Solon T. Kimball. Family and Community in Ireland, Harvard Anthropological Study, 1940, third edition, introduction by Anne Byrne, Ricca Edmondson and Tony Varley. Ennis, Clasp Press, 2005.

Blake-Forster, Charles ffrench. The Annals of Kilfenora or Ye Citie of the Crosses. Galway, The Vindicator (newspaper). Available online, http://www.clarelibrary.ie/eolas/coclare/history/kilfenor a_annals/introduction.htm

Carey, Olive and Clodagh Lynch. Rian na Manach: a guided tour of ecclesiastical Treasures in Co. Clare. Clare County Council, Ennis, 2007.

Dysert O'Dea – a History Trail. Guide and map. [Risteard Ua Cronin] 1989.

Flanagan, John. Kilfenora: a history. Ennistymon Printing, 1991, third edition 2000.

Frost, James. The History and Topography of the County of Clare.
http://www.clarelibrary.ie/eolas/coclare/history/frost/frost.htm

Fletcher, Alan J. 'Liturgy and music in the medieval cathedral', in John Crawford and Raymond Gillespie eds, St Patrick's Cathedral, Dublin. A History, Dublin, 2009, 120-148.

Gerald of Wales [Giraldus Cambrensis]. The History and Topography of Ireland. Trans John J. O'Meara, Harmondsworth, Penguin, 1982.

Graham John. Mason's Parochial Survey, 1814-19, Vol. II, 1816. Union of Kilrush, Killard, Kilfieragh, Moyferta, and Kilballyhone. By the Rev. John Graham, A.M. Late Curate of the Union. Online at
http://www.clarelibrary.ie/eolas/coclare/places/kilkee_history.htm

Griffin, Kevin Anthony (Thesis). Continuity of settlement in counties Limerick and Clare: the role of "ecclesiastical sites" in the formation of settlement. Doctoral, Paper 11. Dublin Institute of Technology 2003,
http://arrow.dit.ie/tourdoc/11/. Section four.

Griffith's Valuation. See Primary Valuation of Ireland.

Harbison, Peter. Pilgrimage in Ireland: The Monuments and the People. Syracuse, University Press, 1995.

Harbison, Peter. "The Church of Rath Blathmach – a Photo-essay", The Other Clare 24 (2000), 23-31.

Harbison, Peter. "An ancient pilgrimage relic road in North Clare?", The Other Clare 24 (2000), 55-9.

Harbison, Peter. "Twelfth-century pilgrims: the Burren's first tourists? Part 2. High Crosses and a 'T' or Tau-shaped crozier reliquary". Burren Insight, Issue 4 (2012), 16-17.

Kalkreuter, Britta. Boyle Abbey and the School of the West. Bray, Wordwell, 2001, 68.

Lalor, Brian. The Irish Round Tower. Cork, Collins, 1999, 2005.

McCaffrey, James. The Black Book of Limerick, Dublin, M.H. Gill and Son, 1907.

MacMahon, Michael. A History of the Parish of Rath, Ennis, 1979.

MacMahon, Michael. "A Burren Church: Killinaboy, Co.Clare". Dublin Clare Association Yearbook 2012.

MacMahon, Michael. The Parish of Corofin – a historical outline, Corofin, 2012.

MacMahon, Michael. "Each Lord in his own Territory: Giolla Na Naomh Ó hUidhrín's profile of Thomond". The Other Clare 36 (2012).

Meaney, Dolores & Jackie Elger. The Islands in the
Fergus Estuary, Quin, Co Clare, Cat Beag Books, 2013.

NFC: National Folklore Collection. NFC 1356. Scattery
Island, Kilrush parish, Moyarta, Clare. Various
informants. Collector Seán Mc Grath, 1954. The National
Folklore Collection, UCD. Used with permission.

Newslink. Magazine of the [Church of Ireland] Diocese of
Limerick.

Ó Cleirigh, N. "The Moravian Brethren and Their Church
at Corofin", The Other Clare, 3 (1979), 27-8.

O'Donovan, John and Eugene Curry. Ordnance Survey
Letters. 1839. Letters containing information relative to
the antiquities of the County of Clare: collected during the
progress of the ordnance survey in 1839. Vol. 2. Edited
Michael O'Flanagan, Bray, 1928.
http://www.clarelibrary.ie/eolas/coclare/history/osl/osl
_index.htm

O'Neill, Michael T. "The architectural history of the
medieval cathedral", in John Crawford and Raymond
Gillespie eds, St Patrick's Cathedral, Dublin. A History.
Dublin, 2009, 96-119.

O'Neill, Michael T. Kilfenora Cathedral. Unpublished
paper, December 2010. Used with permission.

Ó Riain, Pádraig. A Dictionary of Irish Saints. Dublin,
Four Courts Press, 2012.

The Primary Valuation of Ireland [Griffith's Valuation].
1848-1864. For information relevant to County Clare see
www.clarelibrary.ie/eolas/coclare/genealogy/griffiths/
Index.htm

Plummer, Carolus [Charles]. Vitæ Sanctorum Hiberniæ. 2 vols, Oxford, Clarendon Press, 1910.

Plummer, Charles. Bethada Náem nErenn: Lives of the Irish Saints. 2 vols [Irish texts and translations], Oxford, Clarendon Press, 1922.

Plummer, Charles. "The Miracles of Senan", Zeitschrift für Celtische Philologie x (1915), 1-35.

Power, Rosemary. The Celtic Quest: a contemporary spirituality. Dublin, Columba Press, 2010.

Power, Rosemary. Kilfenora: a pilgrim guide. Shannon 2012.

Power, Rosemary. "Iona's sheela-na-gig and its visual context", Folklore 123 (2012), 330-54.

Stokes, Whitley, ed. Lives of Saints from the Book of Lismore. Oxford, Clarendon Press, 1890.

Swinfen, Averil. Kilfenora Cathedral. Drawings by Eileen Whittle. Privately printed, 1986, second edition, 1995.

Westropp, Thomas Johnson. "Churches with Round Towers in Northern Clare", Journal of the Royal Society of Antiquaries of Ireland, xxiv Consecutive Series (1894), 25-34, 150-9, 332-40.

Westropp, Thomas Johnson. "Excursions of the Royal Society of Antiquaries of Ireland, Summer Meeting, 1900: Kilfenora", Journal of the Royal Society of Antiquaries of Ireland, 5th Series, Vol 10, No. 4, 1900, 393-398

Westropp, Thomas Johnson. "The Churches of County Clare". Proceedings of the Royal Irish Academy, Third Series, Vol. VI, No. 1. October 1900, pp. 100-176.

Westropp, Thomas Johnson. "Notes on the Antiquities around Lisdoonvarna, Kilfenora and Lehinch, Co. Clare", Limerick Field Club, iii (1908), 14-29, 91-107, 147-159.

Westropp, Thomas Johnson. "Notes on the Antiquities around Kilfenora and Lehinch Co. Clare", North Munster Antiquarian Journal, Vol 1, No. 2, 1910, 91-107.

Permissions

The author and publisher are grateful for permission to reproduce extracts, including material under copyright, from the following publications. They would welcome information on omissions or inaccuracies.

The Psalms are from the Grail Translation (inclusive version), Harper-Collins, 1993. The Bible translations are from The New International Version (UK edition).

Carney, James. Medieval Irish Lyrics with The Irish Bardic Poet, Portlaoise: Dolmen Press, 1985, 'A wall of forest' 23.

Carney, James, ed. and trans. The Poems of Blathmac son of Cú Brettan, Dublin: Irish Texts Society, 1964, 4-7, 45.

Jackson, Kenneth. A Celtic Miscellany, second edition, Harmondsworth: Penguin, 1971, 'It is folly', 136, marginal note, 177, 'My little hut', 72, 'Sweet little bell', 136.

Kennelly, Brendan, in Patrick Murray, ed, The Deer's Cry, Dublin: Four Courts, 1986, 29.

MacMurchaidh, Ciarán. Three poems, translated by Ciarán Mac Murchaidh, from Lón Anama (Cois Life, 2005) : 'I found my desire', 156-7; 'The Will of God', 135-6; and 'The light of my heart', 246-7.

Meyer, Kuno. Selections from early Irish Poetry, London: Constable, 1911, 'My hand is weary', 89.

Murphy, Gerard. Early Irish Lyrics: eighth to twelfth century, Oxford: Clarendon Press, 1956, 5.

Stokes, Whitley, ed. Lives of Saints from the Book of Lismore. Oxford: Clarendon Press, 1890, for extracts from the Life of Saint Senan.

Waddell, Helen. Mediaeval Latin Lyrics, Harmondsworth: Penguin, 1929, 'Colman', 84-5, 314-5.

#

Lightning Source UK Ltd.
Milton Keynes UK
UKOW02f2238200315

248215UK00003BA/48/P